The Psychology of Smart Investing

The Psychology of Smart Investing

Meeting the 6 Mental Challenges

Ira Epstein
David Garfield, M.D.

John Wiley & Sons, Inc.
New York • Chichester • Brisbane • Toronto • Singapore

AUTHORS' DISCLAIMER

Copyright © 1992, Ira Epstein and David Garfield, M.D.
Published by John Wiley & Sons, Inc.

Library of Congress Cataloging-in-Publication Data

Epstein, Ira
    The psychology of smart investing : meeting the 6 mental
    challenges / Ira Epstein, David Garfield.
        p.   cm.
    Includes index.
    ISBN 0-471-55071-X (alk. paper)
    1. Investments.   2. Investments—Psychological aspects.
    I. Garfield, David   II. Title.
    HG4515.15.E67   1992
    332.6′01′9—dc20   92-436

Printed in the United States of America

10 9 8 7 6 5 4 3 2 1

To my son Max and the rest of my family, and to the man who helped me get started in the futures business, Gilbert H. Miller.

I.E.

To Jake for his ongoing encouragement, and to Jenny, Jacob, Bonnie, Rob, and the extended Garfield family for the same.

D.G.

Acknowledgments

The authors would like to acknowledge the helpful assistance of Tom Marosi in the preparation and coordination of the surveys; to Robin Boesen in the preparation of the manuscript; and Dr. Gina Pingatore for her help in statistical analysis. A special thanks goes to Bruce Wexler for his expert bookwriting and publishing-liaison assistance.

Preface

What happens when you put a psychiatrist and the CEO of a futures firm together? Though this question might sound like the start of a joke, it actually was the beginning of this book. Dr. David Garfield, an academic and practicing psychiatrist, has always been fascinated by the markets. Ira Epstein, head of Ira Epstein & Company, has always been intrigued by the thought processes of investors and traders.

When we first got together about two years ago to discuss how we might combine these two kinds of expertise, we realized that we were on to something; that our knowledge was complementary, and that the sum of that knowledge was greater than its parts. We decided to write a book that would help amateurs and professionals meet the psychological challenges of investing and trading. Our decision was based on the stories we told each other about mind and money—stories that graphically illustrated that it's not what you know that counts, it's how well you know yourself. We were amazed at how very intelligent people lost money in the markets because of mind-created obstacles, and how people of just average intelligence were successful because they had learned how to clear those obstacles.

Neither of us felt competent to write this book on his own. David lacked the intensive exposure to daily trading and investing, and Ira did not possess the necessary knowledge of psychology. But when we put our minds together, valuable lessons about money emerged. We tested our ideas, posing typical problems and opportunities that investors face, and we verbally charted a "mind-over-money" path for them, debating points here and there but generally agreeing on tactics that were sound from both psychological and investing perspectives.

We tested some of our tactics via interviews and surveys, and we were amazed at the results. We found that if you could arm a trader or an investor with the right psychological tools, you could give him a critical edge; you could help him avoid mental blunders and seize opportunities he might have missed if he were less self-aware.

If you doubt this premise, think about the last time you suffered an investment loss and asked yourself: "What's my problem? Why am I losing? How come I can't make more?"

If you are like most investors, your problem may be you. It's possible you're losing because you're unaware of the psychological factors that influence your investment and trading decisions and you're not making more because something inside of you isn't allowing you to do so.

We're not saying you're mentally unbalanced—everyone's view of money is affected by one's particular mindset, regardless of how outwardly "sane" one might be. The objective of this book isn't to "cure" you of what ails you. What you'll read in the following pages is therapy for your pocketbook by way of your brain. If it cures anything, it will be your unconscious tendency to fall short of your potential as an investor or trader.

You see, all of us have psychological strengths and weaknesses. Those strengths and weaknesses determine who you are, and you can no more get rid of them than you can an arm or leg. But you can be aware of them. Once you identify them and realize how they affect your financial performance, you can get them under control. Once your weaknesses are under control, your psychological strengths naturally emerge and help you make a more objective stock, bond, or options move.

To understand how to approach your psychological strengths and weaknesses, we've provided a variety of case histories. You'll find examples of both amateur and professionals investors and how they conquered or were conquered by their particular mindsets. Some of the examples and case histories are about real people. Others are composites. Still others are hypothetical. As much as we would like to provide you only with real histories, we were often dealing with highly sensitive personal issues and respected our interviewees' requests for anonymity and disguising details. Still, even when we changed details, we made every effort to keep the stories as psychologically and financially true to life as possible.

This is a very different sort of book than the ones sitting next to it on the shelves. Unlike those books, this one won't tell you how to sell, buy, or hedge like a pro. It won't provide you with a secret trading formula or a trend-based investing strategy.

But it will give you inside information. More accurately, the book will help you use who you are to your advantage. Most of us forget who we are when we trade or invest. We get so caught up in the markets that we don't even consider our attitudes and biases and how they might be impacting upon our decisions. This happens to grizzled old pros as well as rank amateurs, and we're convinced that any trader or investor can benefit from self-knowledge.

We hope you benefit personally and financially from the mind-over-money concepts contained in this book.

IRA EPSTEIN

DAVID GARFIELD

Chicago, Illinois
May 1992

Contents

CHAPTER 1

The Psychology of Smart Investing

When mental health practitioners talk to patients about their errors in judgment, a typical response is, "I may be crazy but I'm not stupid." Intellectually, these patients know the right thing to do but just can't do it; they can't control their behavior.

The same can be said for investors, most often frustrated by their lack of success. "Little guy" investors and "big guy" brokers, traders, advisors, and planners all bemoan their investing mistakes. They wonder, "Am I naive?" "How could I have made such a patently ridiculous move?" "How in the world could I have thought that stock was going anywhere except down?"

Is everyone stupid? Of course not. That leaves crazy.

MONEY MADNESS

Crazy is a relative term. As one poet said, madness is nothing more than "nobility of soul at odds with circumstance." At the other extreme, there's the crazed killer in

Alfred Hitchcock's movie "Psycho." We see crazy as something different and far more subtle—an attitude of mind that works beneath the surface to frustrate your attempts at successful investing.

If you're like most investors, however, you may labor under the illusion that you're stupid or unlucky. The investment culture has led you to believe that information is the answer. You have to follow all the markets all the time with the latest assessment tools. Such an argument is seductive. After all, the financial world has become interdependent, complex, and global. To play in that world, you have to understand how it works.

Certainly information is important. But you can have all the information in the world at your fingertips and still make mistakes. If you doubt this premise, consider how many times investment gurus wrongly predict the market's direction; consider how many times your broker has given you an unsuccessful recommendation.

Most of you understand the game you're playing. More often than not, you make investment mistakes not because you lack information, but because you *ignore* the information you already possess. You don't follow your systems or pay attention to your indicators because powerful internal forces are at work that stand between you and success.

THE EPSTEIN–GARFIELD SURVEYS

To understand the link between those inner forces and an investor's success (or lack thereof), we conducted a survey of ordinary investors. Those surveyed were not multimillionaire investors; they were ordinary people, men and women, young and old. In the survey, we asked questions about investors' personalities, philosophies, and mind-sets related to their investing.

The results of this survey are as fascinating as they are instructive. We've been able to pinpoint key psychological factors and determine whether they help or hurt an investor's performance. What we learned—and how it applies to you—will be discussed in depth in the next chapter.

We conducted the survey based on our assumption, evolved from years of experience, that an investor's psychological makeup has a tremendous impact on investing success or failure. What we didn't know was how specific personality profiles affected an individual's investing. Would an "obsessive" personality be a better investor than a "competitive" personality, for instance? If we could discover what traits were linked to both gains and losses, we would be able to offer investors a crucial and invaluable edge.

We also conducted a second survey. Here we asked full-time traders, money managers, and advisors to describe their psychological trading world. We asked them what problems have impeded their success? How important are these "inner forces" when it comes to amassing real wealth? And, most importantly, we wanted to learn about specific psychological tools that professionals have found to be key to overcoming inner barriers and unlocking potential. You may find their suggestions both helpful and fascinating.

You'll see how the professionals not only chart the markets, but keep close track of their own inner markets. These tools—a mind/money journal system, personal money timelines, "inner advisors," mentors, and dreams and fantasies—are discussed in a manner that is easy to understand and use on a daily basis. This real "inside" information will allow you to sift through the vast realms of outside data with confidence and direction.

MONEY: A TERRIBLE THING TO WASTE

Everything we learned from the survey has to do with money, and money drives people to do crazy things. In our society, money is more than paper and coins; it's a symbol for everything from self-worth to status. If you fail to understand your personal relationship with money in an investment scenario, you're asking for trouble. Needs for revenge, self-esteem, order, safety, peace of mind, and happiness are all tied to money. If you don't acknowledge and understand these needs, money can drive you crazy.

You have to deal with two marketplaces—one that's "out there" and one that's "inside." Most investors deal competently with the former marketplace and ignore the latter. As a result, they make mistakes with their investments that seem the result of cruel economic forces, lack of investment knowledge, or just plain bad luck.

What they ignore is that, in many instances, the source of the problem is *the investor,* not the market.

THE MEANINGS OF MONEY

Just about everyone wants money, but few know for what. Convenient "what fors" exist: vacations, boats, college educations, homes, jewelry, and so on. Yet, people really want money for deeper reasons. Just as money is a bargaining medium for external transactions, so too is it a negotiating tool for internal deals.

Money has different meanings for different people. Some will say it represents security. Rarely, however, will anyone explain exactly what money is securing. Unknown dangers? Like what? The answer to these questions will help you to realize your own inner needs.

For example, somebody says she needs money because she requires protection against possible health problems. When questioned about this need, the individual responds, "My grandfather had a heart attack and my grandmother went bankrupt paying the doctor bills." Thus, money is security against medical catastrophe: "I'll never let this happen to me."

But what if this person has adequate health insurance? Then money becomes psychological currency, not a real need.

For many frustrated investors, the psychological drive for money might be far removed from reality. Burdened by false perceptions, investors can easily make investing mistakes. No one invests in a psychological vacuum. Everyone has feelings about money—feelings that the investor is often unaware of—and these bias investing strategies.

What Does Money Mean to You?

From our surveys, we found six common feelings about money, including:

1. It's good to have money but bad to want it.
2. Money will make others proud of me and make me proud, too.
3. Money will make me happy.
4. With money, I can beat those who have beaten me.
5. Money keeps me together—without it, I'd fall apart.
6. Having money means I can't get hurt.

Knowing what money means to you allows you to gain control over your money-related behavior. Throughout this book, we'll discuss both the common and uncommon psychological forces that may be controlling you. Those forces include self-esteem and self-image. We'll show you how to make your self-image work for you, not against you.

We will also describe and discuss several "investor/ trader types" or "profiles" that we have identified from our surveys of investors and traders across the country. These types or profiles include "conflicted," "revenging," "masked," "fussy," "paranoid," and "depressed."

We'll also look at our survey results for the personality traits that can affect success and failure. Is there a magical personality type that guarantees financial gain? Conversely, is there a personality type that leads straight to the worst investments money can buy?

To help you get our mind over your money, we'll provide you with the tools that the pros have found useful for moving beyond the inner barriers to success. We'll lay out action plan menus to guide you, and at times, we will ask you to examine your own mind for "inside information." We will give you dozens of examples of how money can control you and limit your chances for success. In each case, we will discuss investor and trader case studies, which will teach you how to break out of your holding patterns and put yourself in control of your money.

RECOGNIZING MIND/MONEY PROBLEMS

Many of you may never have considered the way your psychological state impacts your investments. If not, it's time to start. You don't have to be a psychiatrist to do so. It's simply a matter of making connections between *who* people are and *how* they invest.

This book will give you plenty of practice. Let's start right now with three brief histories of investors. Read them, think about them, try to make connections, and guess the mind-problem that's causing investment headaches. You'll find the correct answers following all three histories.

Case Study

Steven P., An Options Flop

Steven P. is a 27-year-old MBA with a large Boston bank. He works in the bank's currency trading unit and follows the unit's guidelines for cross-currency hedging. He is well respected by his boss and consistently makes the bank a modest but respectable profit. Every year for the last three years, he has been rewarded with both a raise and a bonus.

Last year, Steven started trading stock options for his own account. Given his knowledge of trading and of market behavior, Steven assumed he would duplicate the success he enjoyed on his job for his personal account. All he needed to do was learn a bit about a few, targeted companies and he'd possess all the information necessary to make a significant amount of money.

Steven's dad was an accountant who had made a respectable, if unspectacular, living. He was a partner in a two-person firm with local accounts. Though stern in demeanor and frequently away from home (he worked long hours), Steven's father was good to him. Steven looked up to him and never understood why his father was never more ambitious professionally. His father was charming and funny, and Steven, his sister, and his mother all idolized him and tried hard to please him.

Steven's stock option trading went nowhere. In fact, the first year, he lost $7000—most of his bonus. The second year, he lost $4000. He was upset and commented, "I'm smart and I'm excellent at what I do. Why am I not more successful?"

Steven's lack of success could be attributed to:

A. Obsessive investing.

B. Conflicted investing.

C. Investing to "get even" (revenge).

D. Paranoid investing.

The correct answer is *B*.

Case Study

Alexandra R., An Investment Bookworm

Alexandra R., a married, 33-year-old MBA, is a relatively successful restaurant manager. She and her husband are childless, and her husband has converted their basement into a ceramics studio. He is a talented craftsman and between their two salaries they have saved $30,000. Alexandra has been trying to decide how to invest their savings. After reading a wide variety of financial publications and clipping relevant articles—as well as plowing through almost 50 books on investing— she decided that some of the money should go into mutual funds.

Before investing that money, however, she subscribed to three different newsletters on the subject. They began piling up next to her various books and magazines. In fact, her husband complained that she was encroaching on his studio space and that she should just make a decision.

Finally, Alexandra invested 10 percent of their savings in a stock mutual fund. Once she did so, Alexandra promptly wrote to all 250 companies in the mutual asking for their annual reports.

Alexandra's mind–money problem is:

A. Paranoid investing.

B. Investing for self-esteem.

C. Obsessive investing.

D. Conflicted investing.

The correct answer is C.

Case Study

Brad T., Once Burned, Twice Shy

Brad T. is a retired supervisor/manager for a large electronics manufacturing firm. He now spends most of his time taking care of his suburban home, reading adventure books, and trading silver futures. He was married for seven years, has a son with whom he has little contact, and an ex-wife he never hears from. Brad still remains in contact with several friends he served with during the Korean War.

Brad was reasonably successful in his job, though he disliked his bosses—the firm was sold a number of times, resulting in a rotating series of bosses.

Each day, Brad reads the local newspaper and *Investors Daily*. He also subscribes to a charting service for futures and three separate gold/silver/precious metal advisory services, one of which has a daily hotline. Brad was disappointed in these services and felt he had been burned more than once with "bad" information.

Now, Brad doesn't really trust the news he receives. When his indicators flashed a sell sign for silver, he tried to see if any of his advisory services would confirm the sign, but only one did. Although he thought silver might take a dive, he wasn't sure if he should go ahead and sell. He waited. Silver plummeted. Brad was angry and canceled his subscription to the two advisory services that hadn't advised selling silver.

Brad's problem is:

A. Conflicted investing.

B. Revenge investing.

C. Obsessive investing.

D. Paranoid investing.

The correct answer is *D*.

Whether or not you correctly guessed the problems burdening these investors, you should now have a sense of how the mind affects money. The purpose of this book is to help you determine how your particular mind-set affects your investing and trading.

Through our trader surveys, anecdotes, techniques, and self-tests, we'll give you the necessary tools to help you regain control of your investment decisions.

It's not as difficult as it might sound. Once you acknowledge that you are not completely at the mercy of indifferent marketplace forces, you can begin to take charge of your investing. Once you grasp the connection between who you are and how you trade, you can avoid the insidious forces within that lead you to make "crazy" errors.

The point of this book is not just to assist you in staying away from mistakes. Once you understand your psychological-investor type—and the advantages and disadvantages that accompany that type—you can use that knowledge to create investment strategies and tactics that will maximize your investment potential.

No trading system is foolproof. Every investment carries risk. But when your mind is controlling your money (rather than the other way around), you significantly increase the odds that you'll follow your chosen investment strategy.

CHAPTER 2

The Small Investors Survey

If you're an obsessive person, will that make you a more successful investor? If you're a happy and content individual, will that make you less successful?

Those are just a few of the questions we hoped to answer with the Epstein–Garfield survey. We conducted the survey among 140 ordinary investors who trade stocks, options, and futures. We sent them a detailed questionnaire (see Appendix A) that was designed to give us insight into the relationship between their trading and their psychological makeup.

We classified our survey respondents as "little guys." As opposed to the "big guys"—professional investors/traders—the little guys earn their livelihood from some other occupation. There were 130 men and 10 women, whose ages ranged from 22 to 82. They had little in common except that they invest on a relatively regular basis.

Using statistical methods and with the aid of a computer, we tabulated the results, sifting and sorting the data so that we could interpret it intelligently and pragmatically. Some of the results surprised us. Other results confirmed our assumptions. We expect you'll have similar reactions. The best way for you to understand the survey is to take a "shorthand" version of it that will let you see which mental investing challenge most frequently affects you.

What's Your Investing Profile?

Answer the following questions with a score of 0 to 7 where 0 means "very little" and 7 means "very much." Thus, a score of 4 would mean "not a little, but not a lot." You can use any number between 0 and 7.

---

1. _____ I have been disappointed by my investing/trading systems.

2. _____ I have felt anxious after a successful trade/investment.

3. _____ Unwanted thoughts about trades/investments frequently come to mind.

4. _____ I have been betrayed by my broker.

5. _____ I recheck many times to see if my investment/trade was bought or sold.

6. _____ Investing/trading is a large part of my life.

7. _____ I pull out of losing trades or investments.

8. _____ I am competitive.

9. _____ I take vacations from investing/trading and don't think about it when I am away.

10. _____ I calculate the risk/loss of each potential trade or investment.

11. _____ I am a very orderly person.

12. _____ I am a content person.

This is only about one third of the questions we used in our actual survey, so you should take your results with a grain of statistical salt. They should, however, give you a feel for your profile.

Scoring Key

Add your scores from questions 1 and 6. If the total is greater than 10, it suggests that you may fall into the *revenging* cluster.

Add your scores from questions 2 and 3. If the total is greater than 10, you may fit into the *conflicted* cluster.

Add your scores from questions 4 and 5. If the total is greater than 10, you may fall into the *paranoid* cluster.

Add your scores from questions 7 and 11. If the total is greater than 10, it suggests that you might fall under the *fussy* cluster.

Add your scores from questions 8 and 10. If the total is greater than 10, you may fit into the *masked* cluster.

Add your scores from questions 9 and 12. If the total is less than six, you probably fall under the *depressed* cluster.

SIX INVESTOR TYPES—SIX MENTAL CHALLENGES

1. The Conflicted Investor

If you fit the description of the conflicted investor, you're probably anxious about your trades. Even when you're on vacation, you find your thoughts drifting back to trades, dwelling on the advisability of a move, engaging in debate with yourself about whether the move was wise. During work and other activities, your mind spins with investment analysis—but nothing is clear. When you think about your trading, you feel good about it one minute, bad about it the next. Some days you decide you should invest a lot more money and hold to your strategy; other days, you think you should invest a lot less and try a new approach.

2. The Revenging/Consumed Investor

You can't get enough of the investment/trading scene. You read every financial newsletter you can get your hands on. Investment talk gets you excited like little else. In the back of your mind, you believe that investing can have a profound impact on your life, and can turn it around (as your first true love may have). Perhaps you've suffered some serious losses, but it doesn't dampen your enthusiasm a whit. You come back for more, hoping you'll get even and get better.

3. The Masked Investor

In this cluster, you wish to be an investment superstar. No doubt, you're extremely competitive; winning is everything. Often, you wish to be someone other than yourself; someone bigger or better. Your investment performance is directly related to how you feel about yourself—a successful trade makes you feel like a million bucks, an unsuccessful one is cause for self-doubt. Like a professional athlete, you accept the risks of the game and carefully calculate the odds. When you take a risk, it's a calculated one—you're sufficiently disciplined to avoid throwing it all away on a single play. Each play must be a winning move.

4. The Fussy Investor

Here, you're wrapped up in the process, in the "details" of investing. Are the orders placed correctly? You check and doublecheck. Are they in at the right price? In this cluster, people religiously pore over each trade as if it's a piece of scripture. You won't find anyone in this group with papers spread over a desk or randomly filed. Everything is filed alphabetically, logically, consistently. Orderliness is imperative. To lose track of the details of a trade is a mortal sin.

5. The Depressed Investor

You trade, but there's little pleasure in it. You invest, but whether you win or lose, you're consistently unhappy, discontent, and burned out. If you lose, it just confirms your feelings of inadequacy. If you win, you reproach yourself for not having won more or you attribute it to luck. You seldom give yourself any credit.

6. The Overly Cautious or Paranoid Investor

In this cluster, people keep one eye on their brokers and one eye on the market. You can't be too careful. You're always looking for a way to minimize risk. If you have a system, you don't totally trust it, no matter how well it's done. You rarely, if ever, take a flyer on a new or chancy stock.

WHO YOU ARE, WHAT YOU CAN BE

There will be much more information about each cluster in the following chapters. For now, all that's necessary is for you to get a sense of how your personality relates to your investing. If you're like most people, your personality doesn't fit neatly into a single cluster. Rather, you're a composite of two or three clusters, with a few wild-card traits thrown in.

Focus on the composite. Think about instances when some trait described in the clusters has impacted your investing, either positively or negatively. Perhaps you missed out on a great trade because your paranoia prevented you from accepting your broker's enthusiastic recommendation. Perhaps your obsessive nature enabled you to unearth a buried nugget of valuable investing information. Whatever you learn, the point is to reformulate the way you approach investing and trading. Stop thinking about it in purely "outside" terms (numbers, trends, systems) and start factoring in the "inside" factors (who you are as a person).

Does one cluster seem more attractive to you than another? If your composite doesn't strike you as the optimal one for investing success, don't worry about it. You are who you are, and it's taken you a long time to get there. You're not going to change your personality overnight. It's not possible and it's not necessary. No matter what your composite might be, the crucial thing is to be intimately aware of what it is and what it means. Then you can modify your investing approach to capitalize on the traits that lead to success and watch out for the traits that cause you to make judgmental mistakes.

LOOKING AT THE SURVEY RESULTS

Beyond the clusters, the little guy survey yielded valuable information about investing success (or lack thereof) and such factors as age, gender, and role models. Let's briefly look at what we found.

Age and Personality

Our survey respondents fell into three distinct age groups: below 35, 35 to 55, and over 55. In the last group, Jack C. is 81, retired, lives in Florida, and trades T-bonds using his home computer. In the middle group, Bob S. is 51, works as a pharmacist, and trades a variety of agricultural, currency, and precious metal futures—

two contracts only. Jill S. is a 33-year-old housewife who trades options on stock index futures.

Is the older, perhaps more experienced investor a better investor, drawing on years of investing knowledge? Or is he or she a worse investor, conservative to the point that of shying away from any risk? Is youth an advantage or disadvantage?

Our survey showed us that age has *nothing* to do with success. It was impossible to find any age group that was more or less successful than the others.

We wondered whether the young investors would be more competitive, the middle-aged investors more conflicted, and the older investors more obsessive. Were the common cultural stereotypes accurate: the young, hotshot trader and the older, more conservative investor?

They weren't. Personality types cut across age groups. Sam P., a 77-year-old Chicago retiree, answered questions in such a way that you would think the respondent was an extraordinarily competitive young man willing to take great risks for great rewards. Paranoid types, superstars, and all the other clusters were present in every age group.

Definitions of Success

A critical aspect of our survey was to provide questions that would enable clients to tell us if they were successful or unsuccessful investors. From a purely scientific view, such a method is flawed: There's no guarantee that one respondent's definition of success is the same as another person's definition.

But from our standpoint, we achieved what we sought to accomplish. We wanted to determine whether people *thought* they were successful, not if they were successful on an absolute scale. If investors told us they were highly successful, they went in one category; if they indicated they were very unsuccessful, they went in another. We were trying to determine the respondents' "self-perceived" success—if the investor thought he or she was successful—rather than the general opinion the respondent believed others held of his or her success. This method allowed us to correlate our respondents' perceptions of success with other factors such as age, gender, and role models.

Gender

Though our sample size of women was small, it was sufficient to suggest that there is no correlation between success and gender. Looking at a few, isolated characteristics, we learned that women viewed themselves as no more or less greedy, competitive, paranoid, or aggressive than men.

Role Models

In the survey, we asked people if they had a role model for investing or trading. Of those who considered themselves highly successful, half did.

In and of itself, this fact tells us nothing. But looking at the data in light of the clusters these people were in, two significant pieces of information reveal themselves.

First, the half that didn't have a role model fell into a single cluster: the paranoid/cautious group. From their responses to various survey questions, it became clear that these people had trusted others in the past and been burned. Now, they relied only on themselves, and for them, this self-reliance strategy worked.

The other half with role models fell into a variety of other clusters. For them, reliance on a mentor was crucial. Without the advice or model of others to follow, these people would lower their odds of a successful trade. Thus, if you are a little guy who does not suffer from paranoia, you may do well to have a mentor or role model.

TWO INVESTOR PROFILES

┌───┐
│   *Case Study*   │
│ ┌────────────────────────────────────┐ │
│ │   **Mr. X**   │ │
│ └────────────────────────────────────┘ │
└───┘

Mr. X, who is 42 years old and married, trades commodities part time. Let's take a look at his actual survey responses to see what kind of investor/trader he is. We will also discuss some of his comments.

The following shows some of his responses to the survey. On the 7 point scale (7 is highest, 0 is lowest), he answered 7 to the following questions:

1. Investing/trading is a large part of my life.
2. I have been betrayed by my broker.
3. I have felt relieved after a loss.
4. I am competitive.
5. I am an orderly person.

He answered the following questions with a 5 or 6 (very positive):

1. I become attached to a trade or investment.
2. I can beat the market.
3. I have felt anxious after a successful trade/ investment.

He answered 1 (strongly negative) to this last question:

1. I am a successful investor/trader.

Given his responses, we must conclude that Mr. X has traits of a "conflicted" investor. He is categorized as "conflicted" because he feels anxious after a successful trade, and yet relieved after taking a loss. As you will see in the following chapters, "conflicted" investors will feel relieved by a loss and yet consider themselves to be orderly and competitive. However, the most obvious indicator of Mr. X's situation is that he feels he is an unsuccessful trader/investor.

In a section reserved for comments, Mr. X writes that he feels that he is competitive, yet "inconsistent." In fact, he mentions this inconsistency at least three times. In addition, he sees himself as a "good father, but a poor husband." This reflects a conflicted home life as well. It is evident that conflict stands squarely in the way of his success, both at home and in the market.

Case Study

Mr. Z

Mr. Z is 46 years old, and although he is not a full-time commodities trader, investing and trading are a very large part of his life. He does *not* consider himself a successful trader (answered 1 out of 7). The following list is a sample of his survey responses. See if you can guess what cluster best describes him.

Strongly positive (responded with a 6 or 7):

1. I can beat the market.
2. Bad trades enrage me.
3. I am at odds with myself when I invest or trade.
4. I am competitive.

5. Investing/trading has interfered with my social life.

6. Money is important to me.

In his comments, Mr. Z notes that he grew up feeling deprived—his father was "frugal" and his mother was "cheap." He considers himself a "genius," and states that "he strives to win."

Note the sense of grandiosity and the trouble he has being himself when he trades—his "success-at-all-costs" approach. Mr. Z is a "masked" investor who is blinded by his self-image, his quest, and his efforts to banish the deprivation he felt in the past. However, because he has not accepted who he is, his past is interfering with both his social and financial life.

As you will see in Chapter 12, the problems of the masked investor situation can be remedied, but not until they have been identified and acknowledged.

GETTING TO YOUR GOAL

If you don't know who you are and where you are, you'll never figure out the best way to get where you want to go. *Having* financial goals and having *some* system is not enough. In these times, you've got to know more. You've got to know *who* you are and *where* you are at—otherwise you will be lost at sea—you will be thrown about by the storms of the financial markets.

Who are you as an investor? Can this be classified? Yes, as you've seen you've probably got many traits of one of the six types. That's the first challenge. Next you've got to figure out where you are at—when you read about the professional's survey and discover the navigation tools they rely on, then you can chart your way to success.

CHAPTER 3

The Professional Investors Survey

We conducted a survey among 175 full-time commodity trading advisors (CTAs), money managers, and professional traders to see how they deal with their inner marketplaces. This survey was based on our belief that "little guys" can gain psychological insights from "big guys" in the same way they gain investing tips.

As you'll see from the survey in Appendix B, our questions were designed to learn if professional investors/traders believed there was a connection between their minds and their money. If so, what role did that connection play in their gains and losses? Would their responses mirror those of little guy investors? If their responses were different, what could the little guy learn from that difference?

A startling fact: What percentage of the "big guys" surveyed do you think would agree that psychological or emotional problems have interfered with their trading?

Before we sent the survey, we estimated that no more than 15 percent would make that admission. After all, these are professionals. We assumed many of them would be reluctant to admit to something others might perceive as a weakness.

Surprisingly, 44 percent of the big guys surveyed acknowledged a psychological problem with investing. Almost half the pros felt that they had suffered from internal obstacles to successful trading. So, don't feel bad. It's not what ails you, but how you deal with it that is the key to success in the markets.

Were all the big guys surveyed financial super-stars? Were they people who rarely, if ever, made a bad trade?

Not at all. Though 68 percent of respondents considered themselves highly successful, 20 percent said they were just doing well and 12 percent admitted they were doing badly.

THE TWO BIG PSYCHOLOGICAL CHALLENGES FOR THE PROS

Our survey revealed that most of our professional investors/traders encountered the challenges of two of our psychological profiles at some point in their past: the masked and paranoid types.

The masked investor is driven by a need to maintain an image and to bolster shaky self-esteem. The paranoid investor fears shame and humiliation and doesn't know whom to trust.

Both these clusters suggest a serious lack of self-confidence. Overcoming this lack of confidence is necessary for investing success. Our successful big guys cleared this hurdle. How? By dealing with their doubts and fears. Their comments reflect an acute awareness of their psychological states and a willingness to accept who they are and how it affects their trading.

Perhaps it's easier for a professional rather than a part-timer to confront a lack of self-confidence. For the former, it is his livelihood. For the latter, it's not, even though part-time traders often feel passionate about the markets. Therefore, the professional has greater motivation to confront and overcome whatever may be hampering successful investing.

Our advice to part-timers is to act as if your livelihood depended on your investments and trades. Then, perhaps you'll find yourself bringing your secret fears out into the open.

THE UNSUCCESSFUL 12 PERCENT

Of the 12 percent of respondents who considered themselves to be unsuccessful, half noted traits that fall into our "conflicted" investor profile; the other half divide equally into "fussy," "masked," and "depressed" categories.

Conversely, investors who experienced problems with self-esteem or self-trust rarely described themselves as unsuccessful.

We can draw a few conclusions from this information.

First, if you have a fussy, masked, depressed, or conflicted profile, the obstacles to success as a pro may be more difficult to overcome than if your type relates to self-trust and self-esteem. This is good news for the little guy, the non-professional trader. For the part-time trader or investor who works another job, being conflicted, depressed, fussy, or masked is *easier* for you to deal with and break out of successfully.

Also, we assume that little guys, like big guys, overcome their lack of self-confidence by admitting their feelings and confronting them. From working with and talking to some of these professionals, we've found that they're very open about self-doubts that have cropped up in their past. Rather than suppress their insecurities, they wear them on their sleeves, frequently talking to professional counselors and others about doubts and uncertainties related to their investing prowess.

THE QUALITATIVE RESULTS

In our survey, we provided space for the professionals to comment on the relationship between psychology and successful investing. They could talk about the relationship in terms of themselves or their clients.

Their responses are instructive. They've observed not only their own trading behavior but their clients' behavior in many investing situations. Though we don't have the space to print all their comments here, we've selected different groups of comments that strike us as particularly insightful. Each group offers both professionals and part-timers lessons in mind-over-money investing that we'd like to share with you.

Lesson 1: Never Underestimate What Influences How You Invest

Many professionals noted that they or their clients have made boneheaded moves because they discounted the effect of their personalities on their trades. A few said they forgot how impulsive, egotistical, or cautious they "naturally" were and, as a result, failed to assess how these traits might steer an investment decision in the wrong direction. As one investor said, "When psychology overwhelms intellect and the trading method, losses will certainly result."

Lesson 2: Don't Take It Personally

This is a recurring piece of advice from the big guys. When you lose, don't look at the loss as a reflection of your self-worth (your net worth, yes). Likewise when you win, don't let it "go to your head." Mind and money are connected, but they're not synonymous. You need to establish some distance from your trading. The big guys have. Like doctors and lawyers, they can't afford to become too emotionally involved with what they do or they risk losing their effectiveness. Even if you're not a professional investor, you can adopt a professional stance and outlook. As one of the big guys wrote, "Don't become so personally entwined with your trading and the market that you lose contact with an objective understanding of the emotional dynamics involved."

Lesson 3: Control Your Emotions, Rather than Letting Your Emotions Control You

Control is a common theme for professionals. They use phrases such as "master your emotions" and "don't put yourself at the mercy of your fear of losing" to communicate the importance of control. Some cite examples of how they or their clients foolishly made investing decisions based on emotion. As one said, "Successful trading is not dependent upon forecasting markets or finding better systems. It is dependent upon mastering hope, greed, and fear . . ."

Lesson 4: If You're Greedy, You'll Get Burned

Though professionals are in the business to make money, they don't have unrealistic expectations about how fast they'll make it or how much they'll make. Greed leads to carelessness, which in turn leads to reckless speed in a headlong dash for the gold. Remember, the markets will always be there. You can't be a winner every trading day. An astute pro wrote, "Most people want to make money too fast (a lack of patience), trade too often, and take profits too quickly to get back even. I only trade long term because I believe trading short term is addictive and useless amounts of energy are wasted on short-term trading.

Lesson 5: Be Yourself When You Trade, Not the Person You Think You're Supposed to Be

Our respondents strongly suggest that investing mistakes are made when people follow a system, strategy, or mentor with whom they are ill matched. Some of these professionals talk about how they once tried to adopt the investing style of a boss or guru and failed miserably. Because there is so much mystique and mystery in the markets, people often gravitate to a person or system that appears to make everything comprehensible. Yet, if there is a clash between the investor and his or her model, the relationship won't work. Time and again, we've heard professionals say "you have to be yourself." One respondent put it this way: "I have a trading system that I have tested over the past three years and have proven that it is profitable, yet I can't trade it. My personality and the system don't match. I think that is the most important factor for system traders to be successful. You have to have a system that is compatible with your personality."

Of course, if you are in the "masked" cluster, you are at a greater risk for making the mistake of following a system you are not comfortable with. In the final chapter of this book, we will discuss how to achieve the right distance between you and your money, and how you can strike a balance between you and your systems.

PROFESSIONALS' TOOLS FOR MEETING PSYCHOLOGICAL CHALLENGES

We asked our 175 professionals to name the tools, strategies, and techniques they've used to meet the psychological challenges of successful investing. Here are the five most frequently cited responses. In the following chapters, we'll discuss how you can use each of these tools to meet your personal investing challenges.

The Mind/Money Journal

More than 43 percent of those surveyed commented that keeping a personal journal helped them greatly in dealing with the psychological aspects of their trading and investing. Most investors and traders already chart or track the markets. It is easy to combine this with crucial personal information that will help you manage yourself. Chapter 4 will discuss how to keep a mind/money journal and will detail its benefits.

The Personal and Family Money Timelines

Almost 63 percent of respondents said that charting out their own past successes and failures helped them to understand the psychological aspects of their trading or investing.

They also found that by plotting out a timeline for their family, they were better able to identify their own cycles of success and failure through the historical perspective of their family.

By examining your family's past financial history and patterns, you will gain insight into the traits or characteristics you might have inherited. For example, do you come from a family of entrepreneurs? Were they successful? Did your grandfather lose it all in the crash of 1929? Was he able to recover? In Chapter 5, you will learn how to discover those quiet but powerful forces at work in your family financial tree.

Finding Helpers and Mentors

More than 40 percent of our professional investors mentioned that communicating with "helpful people" was useful in coping with "internal" forces that can lead to losses. Forming strategic alliances with others was a subset of this strategy, and about 30 percent of those surveyed endorsed this technique. We will discuss this strategy in greater detail in Chapter 6.

Paying Attention to Your Dreams and Emotions

A surprisingly large subset of our professionals—20 percent—found that paying attention to dreams and emotions was a very good way to sort through the confusion of the marketplace. Many feel it intensifies the "gut feelings" they often rely on. Chapter 7 details how, by examining your dreams, you can determine what is really on your mind and in your heart. Fears and wishes are exposed for what they are, leaving you less vulnerable to unforeseen trading and investing liabilities.

Constructively "Losing Your Mind"

Your encounters with the marketplace can be exhausting, both mentally and physically. To remain on top of things, you should regularly take time off, get away, or "vacate." Discovering how to rest and refresh your financial mindset in the midst of the clutter of the modern marketplace is more difficult than it may seem. Chapter 8 will help you learn to pace yourself so that you can maximize your investing success.

Now, let's look at how you can use these tools in your investing based on who you are and your psychological type.

CHAPTER 4

The Mind/Money Journal

Navigating the internal marketplace can be tricky. As a trader or investor who is committed to making the odds as favorable as possible, you need the best map you can devise. The first step on this journey is to determine and establish your starting point. You must understand where you are now and where you have been in the past, before you can move ahead. Creating a "mind/money journal" can help you do just that.

Many other tools, which will be discussed in following chapters, were recommended by the professionals we consulted. As our survey shows, most successful professional traders and investors rely heavily on a vast assortment of mind/money tools that help them meet the psychological challenges of the investing/trading environment. Using these tools should help you develop a clear sense of how your personal style, past history, and current preoccupations influence your success.

Now, however, let's focus on the mind/money journal.

THE POWER OF THE MIND/MONEY JOURNAL

Lack of discipline in your approach to your trading systems can be disastrous. What you may not realize is that that same lack of discipline can be just as disastrous when you are trying to gain control over the inner forces that determine your financial moves. It is impossible to keep track of everything in your head. But even on your most hectic days, you can usually find a moment to jot things down to help you stay organized.

But don't jot them down on scraps of paper or in a random fashion.

Use your mind/money journal.

As our second survey shows, many successful traders and advisors rely heavily on a journal to help them navigate the risky investing/psychological waters.

Many, if not most, traders, investors, full-time money managers, and even part-time players keep records, charts, or notes to remind themselves of key events or occurrences, forecasts, or patterns in the marketplace. Record keeping is a natural impulse. We're just asking you to extend that impulse to what's going on inside as well as outside.

Your journal should be for your eyes only. This privacy issue is not minor. The journal becomes a place where you can put down your thoughts, ideas, fantasies, dreams, and plans—all of which have the potential to be embarrassing or revealing. If you operate under the assumption that others will be privy to these innermost thoughts, the freedom to express yourself fully will become restricted. You should safeguard your journal from friends, spouses, children, and colleagues for just that reason. If you don't have the freedom to speak openly within your journal, then it will be hard for the journal to reveal your inner thoughts effectively.

WHAT THE MIND/MONEY JOURNAL CAN DO FOR YOU

We like to think we're in control of our lives. We may enjoy the sense of being in control of our thoughts, feelings, and actions on a moment-to-moment basis. We get up in the morning, somehow the coffee gets made, we get in the car and drive to a destination that we have determined. For all practical purposes, we appear to be masters of our destiny. We feel as if we're in total control.

But it's only partial control. There's a reason why we took Route A instead of Route B to work. On the surface, we might not even question our decision. But something inside us decided that we should take Route A, and we obeyed.

Something inside of us decides that we should invest in Stock A instead of Stock B. If we can determine what that something is, we can control it rather than have it control us.

Like charting the markets, charting in a journal helps give us that control. The recurrent patterns, the formations, the overall direction, the ranges, and the cycles become apparent under "visual inspection." The same is true for your mind and money. Your risk taking, your hesitations, your fears and ambitions, and your hidden self-images—they all emerge and become apparent by "visually inspecting" your journal.

Feedback is critical for success, and a mind/money journal can provide you with that feedback. If you make an investment or a trade that heads south and you wonder, "Did I take leave of my senses when I put my money on that nag?" you can find the answer in your journal.

HOW JOURNAL FEEDBACK WORKS

Suppose two very interesting business opportunities present themselves within six months. One has to do with a new venture, a mail-order business, and the other has to do with buying a large quantity of gold with no premium and no carrying costs of storage. You have the money for both and normally would consider both.

But you haven't acted on either investment opportunity and you have artfully put off the principals of the investments.

You get a call from the CEO of the business venture, who wants to know whether you're in or out. You tell him that you'll call him back in an hour, and you take your mind/money journal and go off for a cup of coffee by yourself. In reviewing your thoughts and notes for the past few months, you realize that you have been preoccupied with your marriage and that, basically, you have put your professional life on hold. The major emotions that seem to be spilling forth are fear and resentment about the lack of affection and physical intimacy —a number of journal entries suggest your dissatisfaction with the sexual aspect of your marriage. You notice that you have been putting all decisions on hold even though you thought that you had been going forward in your work.

One of the things that attracted you to the new business venture was the management team. They are friendly, warm, and competent people who have a good business sense. You review the marketing plan and the financial projections—they seem sound. You have always liked their mail-order idea and believe it could be marketed well. You realize that it is probably sensible to make the investment and that your fear had to do with "getting involved" and risking disappointment in a relationship with "supposedly open and friendly" people.

It's clear from your journal that you've been procrastinating. With the journal's hindsight, you see that you've been putting off the investment for noninvestment reasons. You are now able to appreciate the real investment risk, which is the money and time involved and comment to yourself, "I'm not getting married to these guys—it's okay." You decide to consider the gold investment within the next 10 days.

HOW TO SET UP YOUR MIND/MONEY JOURNAL

The journal may be set up separately or alongside your current market/financial charting system. The best size for a journal is 8½ by 11 inches, since it is big enough to see, yet small enough to fit into a briefcase. Entries should be made chronologically on either a daily or weekly basis. If you use one page for each week, leave an additional page or two blank immediately following the weekly sheet, so that you will have space for more detailed notes (see sample journal on page 36). During any given week, you need to cover four specific areas: events; emotions; thoughts; and dreams, fantasies, and daydreams. You can do this in a variety of ways, such as by setting up columns for each topic area if that seems easiest. The four areas are described in the following sections.

Events

Here you list the key personal or professional events that have taken place. Crucial current events can also be charted. Do not exclude major market reports if they are on your mind. The entry should be made based on what is "on your mind." Or, it should be listed because of an effect that it has had on you in some way or another. People can be included under this category if their actions have had an impact on you. Events ranging from the insurrection of the Soviet Union to an offhand, cutting remark from your secretary are fair game for entries.

Emotions

Try to be as succinct as possible. Most often, the emotions you list are going to relate to an occurrence mentioned in your list of events—but not always! Some people will contend that there are only five or six basic emotions—happiness, sadness, fear, anger, disgust, and surprise. However, just as the Eskimos have 50 words to describe snow, you can use many different words to describe the myriad emotions you experience. Use a variety of terms in your journal. For example, think about the following descriptive words: guilty, resentful, oppressed, hassled, tired, irritated, ecstatic, triumphant, jubilant, mortified, terrorized, insulted, ashamed, downtrodden. All these words could be traced to the six basic emotions we mentioned, but they are far more descriptive and insightful. Rely on such expressive words.

Being able to focus on your exact emotions at any given time allows you to get a better fix on what motivates you. Quite often, emotions are the fuel and force that power and direct your actions. It pays to become acutely aware of what those emotions are.

There will be times when you may feel certain emotions that you cannot link to any current event or interaction in your life. These are particularly important to monitor and record in your journal. Such emotions may have to do with subconscious ideas or fantasies that may be governing your investment or trading decisions.

Thoughts

Keep this section of your journal short, but do keep it. Here you will see what conclusions you draw about events. Small but discernible bits of illogic pour out in the thoughts section. For instance, your secretary barks at you, and you begin to feel harassed and angry. You then decide that your broker is "off by a mile" and that you are not going to buy those 200 shares of Kodak through him. When you write all this down in your thoughts sections—and when you look at it later—you may see the linkage between your secretary's bark and your investment decision.

This section should also include any repetitive thoughts, topics, or concerns that you may have. What keeps swirling about in your mind? Why is it swirling? Can you make a guess? Answer these and similar questions in this section. You can include images here as well, but separate this kind of thinking from wishful fantasy or daydreams, as described next.

Dreams, Fantasies, and Daydreams

What do you fantasize or daydream about while you're awake? What do you dream about when you sleep? Categorize these waking and sleeping dreams as such in your journal, and note the theme of each. You can use the one or two blank pages that follow the weekly entries to provide detail. Here is where your unconscious will speak most directly, though in a somewhat disguised fashion. By labeling the dream or fantasy with a title that refers to its content, you will be able to fit it into the events, emotions, and thoughts matrix that you are assembling in the journal continuously and chronologically.

SAMPLE JOURNAL ENTRIES

Date	Event	Emotion	Thought	Fantasy/Dream
8/28/91	secretary	pissed off	demanding women	dream about seduction

This morning Carol was a real bitch to me. She got back from vacation with her parents and commented that she was in a bad mood—that she had had a great time on vacation and that she hated being back at work. I suspect that things aren't so great with her husband. Just what I needed. There seem to be so many demands to satisfy—it would be nice to feel like someone appreciated what I do. Had a dream last night that a beautiful, dark-haired woman wanted me to come with her on her boat. It definitely had sexual overtones. She was beckoning me. Sarah seems to be so preoccupied with her career that she forgets that she is also my wife—I feel I'm only there to support her, make sure the money is there, and not complain. Makes me feel pressure to trade and bring home winners.

Date	Event	Emotion	Thought	Fantasy/Dream
8/30/91	new contract	hassled	too much work	vacation house

I'm happy we got the new contract for the software, but it means my life for the next few weeks will be crazy. There is so much work to be done with it. Gold should be in for a nice fall soon. If it didn't skyrocket after the failed Soviet coup attempt, then only a governmental emergency here in the U.S. will make it happen—or, skyrocketing inflation, which won't happen until we go into a more serious recession and the FED prints tons of money. In the meantime, bonds should do quite nicely, but I've go to be able to get out of them easily. Probably just going long futures with a far-out expiration will do the trick, but I've got to research the current status of the bond market overall, considering that some of the major banks are so close to the edge and their paper may become worthless. So, when am I going to have the time to do this? Somehow, I keep seeing that little cabana house in Costa Rica in that magazine ad—I bet something like that could be had for less than $10,000.

Date	Event	Emotion	Thought	Fantasy/Dream
9/1/91	Mom on phone	pleased	where's Dad?	car crash dream

I spent two hours talking my mother into buying a new dress for herself. This is crazy—ridiculous. She really appreciated my encouragement—that she

should go ahead and get it. It felt good to be appreciated, but I didn't get to talk to my broker about the
bond market, didn't get to work on the new contract.
How come Dad didn't get her to buy the new dress?
Yet, he seemed pleased that I helped her, too. Who is
helping me? Gold closed at 351 and T-bonds were
down to 89 even. FED put money in in the morning.
Then I have this incredible nightmare about driving
along the Santa Monica Freeway to Costa Rica and all
of a sudden, the car loses its steering and is about to
crash into a viaduct. I think I must be worried about
having so much going on that I'm gonna lose it. I'll
talk to Jack tomorrow about the bonds, but I think
I've got to get out of here for awhile and take a break.
Maybe I can talk Sarah into taking some time away.
We both need it badly, and it would help our marriage. Desperately need to unwind. I'm not sure this is
the best time for me to trade—first, I've got to clear
my head. Then I'll take a look at the bond futures. I
really need more time to trade properly.

I still can't believe I spent half the day on my
mother's dress. Am I that guilt ridden? Pathetic.

USING YOUR JOURNAL ENTRIES

The individual who made these journal entries is a conflicted investor. He is employed as a software designer.
Obviously a very busy man, he's involved with his family, trying to do right by everyone. He is sorting out what
he is going to do in the markets, has some good ideas
about the bond futures market, and has his eye on gold
down the line.

Yet he is unable to act. He is so caught up with trying
to please everyone and be appreciated that he doesn't
carve out time for himself. He has not set aside time for
his trading, either. But he has realized that he needs time
away from his usual hectic pace—time for himself.

His dream tells him that he is feeling seduced by
someone who appreciates him. This need is driving his

behavior—he spends a lot of time in a trivial effort surrounding his mother's dress. This need to be appreciated interferes with his ability to make time for himself.

The journal reveals that the fantasy about the house in Costa Rica is on his mind a lot lately. He connects the image of the house with taking a vacation. His dream about the car crash on the way to Costa Rica connects his fantasy of taking a vacation with the underlying guilt he feels when he does not meet the demands of all the people in his life.

Quite nicely, he realizes from reviewing his journal that he needs a break. This will give him some much deserved and needed time away to regain his energy and, perhaps, to revise his schedule so that he will have enough time to set up his trades properly. He also sees it as an opportunity to regroup with his wife and possibly repair some of the damage done to their relationship. If successful, this would relieve some pressure and allow him to devote more energy and mental capacity to trading. He notes that trading right now would be a bad idea; he views it as an added pressure of having to "bring home the bacon" that his family requires. Waiting to trade until he is back from vacation is definitely a good idea. The journal puts it out for him to review and make a decision.

The journal isn't a crystal ball. The software designer in our example didn't merely gaze at it and find all the answers. Like any tool, it takes time and practice to use it well.

Perhaps our best advice is to look at what you've written as clues in a game. Everything isn't spelled out. Like the software designer, you have to make connections on your own. You're going to have to make some guesses.

However, with practice, more often than not, you'll guess right. If the only thing our software designer learned from his journal was that now was not the right time to trade, he would have learned something valuable.

But because he was well-versed in the ways of his journal, he discovered an even more important piece of information: If he relaxed and regrouped, he would gain the mental and physical energy essential to good trading.

Remember, too, that the journal is not your only mind/money tool. If you use it and nothing else, you will be putting yourself at a disadvantage. If, however, you use the journal in conjunction with the tools described in the following chapters, the journal will tell you much more about your investing/psychological connections.

CHAPTER 5

The Personal
Money Timeline

To conquer money and make it work for you, one of your most valuable weapons is the personal money timeline. Our survey of professional money managers and traders showed that learning from past patterns—both positive and negative—is critical to your future success. More than 75 percent of full-time traders and investors report that identifying recurrent patterns of successes and errors was a key tool in overcoming the psychological obstacles to successful investing.

You look for recurrent patterns every day in the cycles, graphs, and movements of stocks, options, and commodities. Now it's time to look for them in your own actions. This is where you can really get a grasp on what will and what won't work for you.

On a clean, blank piece of paper, plot out your life in five-year blocks (age 0–5, 5–10, 10–15, 15–20, 20–25, etc.) across and down the page. You may do this in your journal or separately. Under each segment, jot down the critical aspects of your life during that phase, paying particular attention to your financial condition and circumstances.

For example, in your entry for the phase between the ages of 0–5, you might note the following:

- Family had little money
- Living in an apartment
- Dad envied Uncle Bob's lucrative law practice
- Parents saving for a house

Keep it brief, but keep it salient. You will also want to note the prevailing economic condition during that time; for example, recession, recovery, savings & loan fiasco, runs on credit unions. This puts your personal money timeline in sync with the global money timeline.

PATTERNS OF SUCCESS AND FAILURE

Identifying recurrent patterns of success and failure is key to overcoming psychological obstacles to investing. Each investor and trader must examine specific patterns, but what are they?

Look at your timeline for the following:

1. Which investing and trading vehicles have been most profitable: real estate, art, stocks, bonds, gold/silver, commodities, options, or new business ventures?

2. Within and between the larger vehicles, which strategies have been most or least profitable? Puts? Calls? Bull spreads? Bear spreads? Buy/writes (long stock, sell the out-of-the-money call option on the stock; long futures, sell the out-of-the-money call option on the futures—or the reverse, with shorting and the corresponding puts)? IRAs? Keoughs? Zero-coupon bonds?

3. Which risk/reward ratios have been most or least profitable? High risk/high reward? Low risk/moderate reward? Moderate risk/high reward?

4. Which currency has been most or least profitable for you to risk on trades or investments? Cash? Savings?

Equity? Windfall (unexpected) money? Reputation? Time? Don't forget—time is money . . . the time spent following any given market or put into a new business venture could be earning dollars in some other way.

5. Which investment "formats" have been successful? Format is the administration of the investment or trade. Are you a floor trader? A trader at your home computer? Do you use a broker? Do you place the trades yourself? Do you use a money manager? Do you invest through an investment club? Do you have a trading, investing, or business partner?

Find the patterns. If you're diligent about creating your timeline, I suspect you'll be startled by what you discover. Perhaps you'll find that high-risk, high-reward investments always turn out well, and low-risk, low-reward ones always turn out poorly. It might be that you generally do well with stocks and poorly with bonds.

Whatever the pattern, pay attention to the implications. Perhaps the best way to understand how to spot the implications is through Ed's story.

Case Study

Ed E.'s Edge

Ed E. is a 40-year-old internal medicine specialist, earning $100,000 per year. His wife Mary works as a nutritionist, earning $27,000 per year. They have two children, ages seven and four. Ed and his wife live fairly well, and while they are not extravagant, they indulge themselves occasionally—they travel at least once a year without the kids for 10 days and take a family vacation every summer to either California, Cape Cod, or the Caribbean. Their house is not huge, but it also doesn't carry a huge mortgage.

Ed has tried a variety of investing and trading strategies to boost his income and net worth. He had traded stocks and has dabbled in options. He works extra hours to increase his income through moonlighting and has cut back on expenses to save money. He has used two different commodity advisors, and he and Mary have started their own small business—a nutrition/health newsletter geared toward the parents of school-age children.

Before we discuss which of these tactics have worked or failed to make money for Ed, let's outline his personal money timeline.

Ed's Personal Money Timeline

Age 0–5 (1951–1956). Dad worked for General Electric as a production manager. Family moved to an apartment in an upper middle-class suburb on Long Island. Mom was raising three kids. Family rarely ate out, but took a two-week vacation every summer at a nearby beach resort that was sparse and inexpensive, but fun. Family decided not to own a car, so Dad took the train. Money was never discussed.

Age 5–10 (1956–1961). Ed's father becomes general manager of the plant. Ed remembers asking for an expensive Lionel train set and Dad responded with, "I have to make two dollars for every one dollar you spend." Mom would talk about the nice houses owned by other families on Long Island. Ed had many friends who lived in big houses, and their parents would take him along when they went out to eat. His friends also have elaborate toys—trains, sailboats, and lots of sports equipment. His parents frequently talk about the need to save more money to send his two older brothers to college.

Age 10–15 (1961–1966). Ed spends a lot of time with wealthy friends. Starts his own summer business with one of them, selling hot dogs at a nearby beach. The business lasts for just one month, but they make money and have fun. The plant that Dad works at is threatened with closure—Dad is worried about his job. Dad gets into the stock market and loses several hundred dollars. Mom doesn't complain. Dad always at work, never around much. Dad wants all the boys to become professionals. Never takes them to the plant, which stays open. Good grades are constantly stressed. Mom starts a part-time job at a fancy department store as an assistant buyer.

Age 15–20 (1966–1971). Ed is expected to make money each summer to help pay for college. He works as a nurse's aide in a nursing home and decides that he'd like to go to medical school someday. One of his older brothers is preparing to become a CPA, and the other one is thinking about clinical psychology. Ed's parents decide to stay in the same apartment so that he can go to a private college. Dad and Ed had hoped he would get accepted at Princeton, but he doesn't. Ed gets into Oberlin, which the family thinks of highly. His parents begin to talk about moving into a condo in a beautiful complex in a nearby town.

Age 20–25 (1971–1976). In addition to his summer job, Ed works one night a week during school. He gets into a New York State medical school located downstate and borrows tuition. His parents cosign the loans. Ed studies hard, lives on next-to-nothing, and has many friends. Mother is quite successful in her job and gets promoted to buyer. Dad continues to do well as general manager of the plant. Parents get the condo they wanted. Ed considers money to be relatively unimportant in his life.

Age 25–30 (1976–1981). Ed enters internal medicine residency and begins to pay back $200 per month on his loans, which now total $40,000. This only leaves him with $700 per month to live on, which is okay by him. His older brothers tell him that the folks should help him more with his loans. Dad had paid off $15,000 of his older brother's loans for graduate study in clinical psychology. Ed doesn't want to ask. Ed meets Mary, who was working as a day-care teacher. Mary would like to get a master's degree in nutrition. They get married, Ed finishes his residency, and he takes a job in an HMO in Great Neck, New York. Ed and Mary rent an apartment. Mary starts graduate school. Ed is still paying back his loans, and money is tight. Ed starts moonlighting at a "Doc in the Box" freestanding ambulatory care center near their home. Dad offers to help repay some of Ed's loans. Even though Ed agrees, he doesn't like taking the money because of his pride.

Age 30–35 (1981–1986). At age 33, Ed has his first child, Melissa. Buys a small house in Great Neck, where real estate values are going up. Mary stays home with the baby—she completes her degree in nutrition. Ed is constantly working and rarely home. He wonders if he can do better in the stock market than his father did at this age. He studies it intensely. Trades stocks in his IRA, which has about $15,000 in it. Learns about options and trades some of them as well. Ed does well when he trades spreads, but poorly when he buys puts or calls alone. Does well with individual stocks making moderate moves but feels he doesn't have enough capital to make much money except through options. Loses almost all of his speculative capital on puts and calls within a two-year period. Mary doesn't complain. Has an inferior broker who gave him bad advice and told him to trade in his IRA but doesn't blame the broker. Just feels stupid and slightly humiliated. Increases his moonlighting. Suddenly, money is important to him, even though he doesn't like that idea.

Age 35–40 (1986–1991). Ed is still working at HMO and moonlighting. Torn between getting a group practice job, which might get him a bigger salary, or staying at the HMO, where he likes the fixed hours because he can spend more time with Melissa. But then again, he still moonlights a lot and isn't home very often. Ed reads about commodity trading advisors who make 100 percent per annum on investments. Gives $15,000 that he has put together from moonlighting to a CTA. Has a second daughter, named Jennifer. Mary begins working part time at a nearby hospital but takes four months off when Jennifer is born. Ed goes up and down with the CTA and, after two years, has lost $10,000 of the money he had saved. His parents give each child $5000 for a college fund. Mary starts working full time when Jennifer is two years old. Ed's salary at the HMO has gone up progressively, and he becomes the medical director at the HMO branch where he works. Ed stops trading stocks and commodities, wondering whether he's just like his dad, fearing he will lose if he tries. He and Mary put together a newsletter on nutrition for parents of school-age children, which looks promising.

What Does Ed's Personal Money Timeline Reveal?

1. Ed's Successful Vehicles and Strategies
   A. Trading individual stocks with moderate price moves.

     B. Option spreads.

     C. Extra jobs (moonlighting).

     D. Moving up in his own field (increases salary as medical director).

     E. New Business. Was successful as a teenager. Time will tell whether the newsletter will be a success.

2. Ed's Unsuccessful Vehicles and Strategies

     A. Puts and calls alone (lost almost $15,000).

     B. Money managers or brokers (both stocks and commodities).

3. Ed's Risk/Reward Ratios

     A. Low risk, moderate reward (stock trading) and buy/write strategies were successful.

     B. Low risk/high reward—puts and calls—were unsuccessful.

     C. High risk/high reward—commodity trading advisors—were unsuccessful.

4. Ed's Subtype of Risk/Reward Strategies

     A. Using his time to make money was successful (moonlighting, possibly the newsletter?).

     B. Using all long-term savings was unsuccessful.

5. Ed's Trading Formats

     A. Using a broker/money manager has been unsuccessful.

     B. Having a business partner has been successful (both as a teen and with his wife).

     C. Solo investing may work out well also.

Conclusions from Ed's Timeline

1. Ed is most likely a conflicted investor. He is competing with his father, and yet fears "being just like him." This has cost him. He also has some traits of the overly cautious or paranoid investor because of being humiliated by losses and by accepting help to repay his school loans.

2. As a conflicted investor, Ed would benefit from not trying so hard to outperform his father, but rather by focusing on his own lifestyle and his wishes for his family. He needs to identify the reasons he wants to increase his net worth—he likes to travel, for instance. Then, the extra money (besides what he needs for retirement and his children's college education) may be saved for a summer home or for exotic trips. This would be the goal behind his efforts—a goal Ed needs.

3. The money timeline tells Ed that he does best without a money manager or broker. This is true of many paranoid investors.

4. Ed does better with low- or moderate-risk/high-reward strategies: buy/writes and trading stocks that do not have extremely high Betas (volatility). He might do well with low-to-moderate-risk commodity strategies, such as the TED spread or going long futures—buying a slightly out-of-the-money put on the futures and selling a farther out-of-the-money call on the same futures. These have moderate reward potential.

5. Ed is smart to try this business venture with his wife— low risk (a time risk mostly) with moderate reward. It also allows him to spend more time with his family, which is something that he missed when he was growing up. This venture is also a wise idea because he has worked well with others through this sort of strategic alliance in the past (the hot dog business).

DRAWING YOUR OWN CONCLUSIONS

We'd advise you to follow the two-step process we used with Ed when you analyze your own timeline: (1) Jot down your success and failures with money from each timeline segment, categorizing them according to the financial areas we mentioned earlier (risk/reward, trading format, etc.). (2) Make logical assumptions about your strengths and weaknesses as an investor, allowing the past to be a guide to what you should do and not do in the future.

If this two-step process seems insufficient or if you're unable to draw useful conclusions from your timeline, here's a timeline interpreter that should facilitate the process.

THE TIMELINE INTERPRETER

- What's the smartest thing you've ever done with money? What's the stupidest? Look at your timeline and write down these two "extremes." Under each of them, list other, less extreme smart and stupid actions that are of the same type. This is an alternative way to spot patterns in your investing/trading approach.

- Review our psychological/investment clusters and determine which one is most reflective of your actions and attitudes toward money. Have you been paranoid about money most of your life? Conflicted? If the timeline helps you pinpoint a cluster, turn to the chapter about that cluster and follow the recommendations there.

- Project your timeline 5 or 10 years into the future. If you continue your current patterns, what might happen with your investments and other financially related matters for the next time period or two? Be logical and realistic. Looking at your timeline, what would you expect to occur next? Write down your projections. What patterns do you have to sustain to make the successful financial moves come true? What patterns should you change to avoid the failures?

MONEY IN THE BLOOD

Your attitude and actions related to money are not only determined by your personal timeline; your family timeline plays a role as well. Many of you may go through the exercises we recommended and find that there's a piece missing. You look over your timeline, and your money moves seem out of sync with the person you perceive yourself to be. Maybe you have a history of being very cautious with money, yet every few years or so, you take some outrageous gamble on a stock, the ponies, or a real estate property. Your impulsive and uncharacteristic gamble seems to come out of the blue.

In many cases, it may come out of your family history. Perhaps your great-grandfather was a riverboat gambler; maybe your dad loved his high-stakes poker games more than anything he did at work.

Whatever the scenario, you can no more escape your family's approach toward money than you can flee from the genes you inherited. It's inside you and plays a role that can be subtle or obvious. In the latter case, it may be that you come from a family of penny-pinchers, and that background translates into your unwillingness to invest in anything but "sure things." The subtle influence, on the other hand, might result in the following situation: You come from a wealthy family that has always been involved in philanthropy: Your parents and grandparents have always believed that it is their duty to spend a considerable amount of time, effort, and their personal fortune to help those less fortunate than themselves. It could be that such an attitude has had a negative effect on your trading; you may have placed an unconscious "stop" on your profits. A large profit triggers guilt; the prospect makes you want to "give something back" to the less fortunate.

Whether subtle or obvious, it's important to maintain a family as well as a personal money timeline.

THE FAMILY MONEY TIMELINE

Use your family tree as the structural basis for your family money timeline. Starting as far back as you can go, use the standard genogram format to separate the generations of your family. Use circles to represent women and squares to represent men. Draw a diagonal line through the circle or square if that person is deceased. Connect the circles to squares with a line to indicate marriage. If the marriage terminated in divorce, draw a diagonal line through the connection. From the middle of the marriage line, draw a line down to the next level to represent the children of the next generation.

For each person in the timeline, characterize his or her relationship to money in the following ways:

- *Attitude.* Were they spendthrifts or cheap; did they love money for money's sake or for the things it bought; was money a driving force in their lives?
- *Talent.* Did they have a particular skill with money; was Grandpa a whiz with stocks; was Grandma a great saver; did Dad go to Vegas and regularly come out ahead?
- *Job.* What did they do to make money; did they make a lot of it?

Do you see a pattern in the characteristics that's duplicated in your personal money timeline? Is there a particular person in your family whose financial profile elicits a strongly negative or positive reaction; if so, why are you reacting that way?

Figure 5–1 will give you a better sense of how a family money timeline might look.

USING YOUR TIMELINES

Using the tools of the personal and family money timelines will allow you to draw on the lessons of the past for better financial performance in the future. You can learn the money-related traits you inherited as well as uncover patterns in your own investing/trading history. Just as you look for those recurrent three advancing waves up

Figure 5–1 Ed's Family Timeline

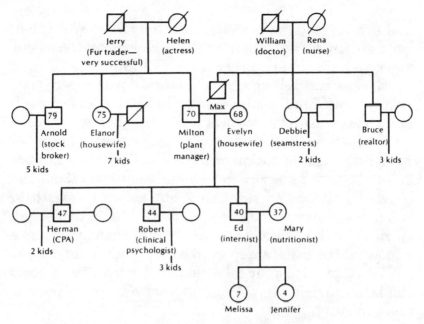

Grandfathers and Grandmothers

Jerry and Helen: A successful fur trader in Canada. Madly in love with beautiful actress, *Helen;* divorced when Ed's father, Milton was 6 years old; Jerry lost all his money—family doesn't know how.

William and Rena: Very successful doctor in Detroit—married his nurse; very conservative with his money; gave it all to his kids even though he never amassed very much.

Aunts and Uncles

Arnold: Go-for-broke stockbroker. Always felt his little brother Milton was too conservative; wonderful and attentive to Ed; Tumultuous marriage.

Elanor: Loved to marry rich men—they always seemed to die; seven entrepreneurial children.

Debbie: Hard-working, talented seamstress.

Bruce: Acquired real estate slowly; very thoughtful.

Family Summary

Conservative and Entrepreneurial forces. Risk-oriented members were more available to Ed yet slow but steady businessmen seemed ultimately more successful. Fur trading and stock trading might have been okay in context of stable family life.

and two corrective waves down in the Elliot Wave five-wave structure, you also need to see how old patterns put you on a path toward either success or failure.

Equally compelling are the historical patterns of your family. Both fundamental and technical traders consistently make use of historical data, whether it concerns trends that occur during an election year or market behavior during a recession or recovery. They then can position themselves accordingly. Family patterns should be charted and studied similarly. Your elders bequeath to you not only money but their passions, fears, talents, and spirit as well. Capitalize on the best of that inheritance and avoid the black sheep of your financial family.

Together with your mind/money journal, these tools can help you meet the psychological challenges of trading and investing.

CHAPTER 6

Finding Helpers and Mentors

What if you feel overwhelmed by the psychological challenges you face? What if your particular mind/money cluster (or clusters) is like a straitjacket? What if you feel as if you can't escape the effect of who you are on how you invest.

In other words, what if you can't hack it by yourself?

Then consider the tool of finding helping people. As you'll recall, a significant finding in the Epstein–Garfield survey of professional money managers and CTAs was that they often rely on "other helpful people" to overcome internal barriers to success. What do we mean by "other helpful people"? Where do you find them?

PSYCHOTHERAPISTS AND COUNSELORS

When you engage the services of a psychotherapist or counselor, you are hiring a professionally trained consultant to help you discover those internal patterns that inhibit, as well as promote, your ability to succeed.

Psychiatrists, psychologists, social workers, clergy, and psychiatric nurses all have the requisite training and education, but some are better suited to your situation than others. While few psychotherapists specialize in working with investors and traders, those that do may be particularly helpful for your problem or circumstance. To find the right person for your needs, interview such professionals as you would a job candidate. Familiarity on their part with the financial world will be advantageous. Ideally, the person you choose will understand what you want to get out of your sessions and agree that it's possible to achieve those goals.

To clarify exactly what you want, ask the prospective helper the following three questions:

- Can you help me identify the type of psychological investor I am?
- Will you be able to help me determine how my goals, drives, talents, and defenses work for and against me?
- Will you be able to link my personal and family history to my investing/trading decisions?

If a therapist answers these questions affirmatively, you may have found someone who can have a positive effect on your investing.

Varieties of Psychotherapy

Psychotherapy is not an exact science, and a therapist may employ any one of many theories and schools of thought. Some approaches are grounded in the analysis of behavior: They examine how you make your decisions (the steps that you take before making a trade, for instance).

Some therapists are dynamically oriented. They look at the mistakes you repeat, with the hope of determining and correcting the cause of that pattern. The *dynamic* approach attempts to foster insight into your behavior, which allows for change; the *behavioral* approach doesn't care why you do what you do, but only that you keep doing the good things while avoiding the bad. Some therapists combine the two approaches.

Psychoanalysis is an in-depth, dynamic approach that looks intimately into your past and present. Your patterns of action are gently put under your own microscope. You dreams and fantasies are looked at carefully. Your relationships are investigated respectfully. Certain motivations that may be specifically throwing you off track can be clearly crystallized and grasped. Fears of success or failure come out of the closet. Hidden self-images reveal themselves.

Which approach is right for you? One way to answer that question is to think about the investing problem you wish to correct.

If you're totally mystified about your trades—if it seems as if someone else is calling your investing shots—then psychoanalysis might best meet your needs.

If you recognize a clear pattern in your investing that results in losses—if you always seem to put your money into a stock at its peak, just before it heads down—then the dynamic approach might suit you.

If there's a zigzag pattern to your investing—if you win some, then lose some—you might want to consider a behaviorist, who can keep you focused on how to make better investment decisions.

When to Use a Psychotherapist

- You can't work through your psychological obstacle or challenge on your own.
- You're confused and concerned by your investing behavior—it seems as if a stranger is making the trades, and the stranger is losing.

- You've identified yourself as being in one of the clusters identified in later chapters of this book, but you don't know how to escape the investing pitfalls of that cluster.

HELPERS IN YOUR EXTENDED FAMILY

You might be surprised at the wealth of talent and experience that exists within the extended network of a family, particularly in relation to investing and trading. Ironically, most people don't look for help within their own extended family tree.

By extended family, we mean to include not only pure blood relatives, but that special set of people we call "friends of the family." These are the "aunts" and "uncles" who aren't really related to you, but who lived next door to your parents for years or who knew your dad when he was in the army. Not only might your real Uncle Bob know a great deal about the gold coins, but your Aunt Sally, who was Mom's roommate in college, may work at the CBOE (Chicago Board Options Exchange) and be close friends with the president of the exchange. You need to find out what is going on within your larger family to see whom you know and how they might be helpful to you.

We can provide a telling example of this kind of extended family. The three of us who are responsible for this book consider ourselves to be an "extended family." We—David and Ira—are figurative cousins, even though there is no blood connection. Ira's ex-wife, Liz, grew up next door to the Garfields, and the families have remained close over the years. Additionally, the book's agent and writing consultant, Bruce Wexler, is also a "cousin" because David and Bruce's fathers have been best friends since childhood. This is how a psychiatrist, a commodities trader and stock/option broker, and a literary agent have come together as helpful collaborators and partners on a book project. You don't have to be in a syndicate to find helpful people within your extended family.

When to Use Your Extended Family

- You don't feel comfortable talking about your problem with anyone outside of your family circle.

- You have someone in your extended family who has always helped you discover things about yourself.

- Someone in your family has expertise or experience in an investment arena relevant to you and also knows you well enough to give you a unique combination of investment/psychological advice.

Case Study

Regular Time with Friends

Alan Is a 29-year-old vice-president of a small paint company in Pittsburgh. He is also an avid stock options trader. He is married, and holds a BS in chemistry. After college, he took a job as a chemist for a specialty paint company. He gets along quite well with the owners and, after a few years, found that he enjoyed both management and business in addition to the technical aspects of his job. Soon he was not only improving quality control in the production process but also substantially increasing the amount of contact he had with customers. He showed a definite business aptitude, and the owners sent him to a three-week small business workshop at Harvard University. When he returned, Alan was able to automate much of the quality control process for paint color matching. Last year, he was promoted to vice-president of the company, a fairly remarkable move for someone his age.

Two years ago, Alan decided to take 10 percent of his income and try to boost his personal assets. He took night courses on the stock market and options trading at a nearby business school. He decided to trade both deep-in-the-money and far-out-of-the-money puts and calls. He chose the underlying stocks to trade by reading *Barron's* and tried to predict which companies might take off and which would likely encounter trouble. He looked at insider purchase and sales figures and made some choices based on that information. All in all, his trading performance turned out to be pretty poor. Most of the stocks he picked to go up peaked shortly after he bought them and then pulled back and the ones he shorted did not seem to go down.

With three children, his wife, his demanding job, and his foray into the stock market, Alan found himself with little free time. He was particularly upset about his escalating weight, which he couldn't seem to get under control. He needed to lose at least 20 pounds. He had also lost touch with many of his old high school and college friends who still lived in the area.

Then Alan ran into George, a close friend since high school, at the supermarket. Although they had once been very close, they had not seen each other in six months. Because they both had their children with them, they found it difficult to talk, so they decided to go and have a cup of coffee at an ice-cream parlor where the kids would be occupied. It took them about 20 minutes to realize that they were in the same predicament—they both had no time for friends and really missed each other.

George, married with two kids, worked as a chiropractor in his own private practice. He hadn't done much investing but was thinking of putting some money into a new business venture. When Alan mentioned that he was thinking of joining a local health club because it was summertime, and memberships were inexpensive, George decided to join, too. They made plans to meet every Friday afternoon at 3:00 to work out, followed by a cup of coffee at a nearby cafe where they could talk. That left them plenty of time to be home for dinner with their families.

During their workout, George and Alan were able to discuss with each other the events and activities of the week, and their sessions turned out to be very valuable brainstorming time. For example, George pointed out that Alan knew a great deal about the chemical and paint industry—he knew which companies were doing well, and which were failing, and he knew how the business cycle affected that particular industry. He would question Alan about specific companies, and Alan would use those stocks for his options trading. Alan agreed that he was being led astray by relying strictly on outside sources, such as *Barron's,* when he knew a lot about many listed companies through his own experience. Many of these companies had listed options for trading as well. Alan's investing performance improved dramatically due to this simple suggestion from George.

Alan, in turn, cautioned George not to join the new venture he was considering until it became clear that the management team was very, very solid. George went back to the principals and asked some hard questions, which resulted in some significant additions being made to the management team to broaden their marketing expertise. George was able to learn about basic business components from Alan. On top of all that, they both got into great shape.

This strategy of spending time with friends, using them as a sounding board, and serving as a sounding board in return, is consistent with the major principle in finding "other helpful people"; a collaborative, alliance-based approach is best. You are still doing it alone, but it is as though you've assembled your personal advisory board to consult with before making your own decisions.

When to Use Friends

- You're having problems with your investing, and there's a friend who has known you long and well and who may be able to offer a more informed perspective about the cause of the problem than anyone else.

- You have a friend who seems to need your help as much as you need his or hers.

- You receive helpful investment/psychological advice from a friend by accident. During the course of a conversation, the friend comments on a particular trading problem you've had, and the suggestion or insight strikes you as right on the mark. You may want to make it a habit to seek such advice and insights from this friend.

HELPERS AT WORK

Colleagues

Full-time professional traders find mastering money with their mind sometimes requires regular consultation with other full-time money-managers and traders. The same principle applies to part-time traders and investors. You'd be surprised at the number of people you work with who are actively involved with the markets on a part-time basis. Many of these co-workers may also have similar emotional and psychological forces to deal with in their investing and trading and can provide you with valuable insights and techniques for coping with the complexities of internal and external investing indicators.

Case Study

Steve and John

Steve and John are about the same age, and both are salesmen at the same automobile dealership. They had both been there for about three years, yet each had no idea that the other was active in the stock market. Steve as a "consumed-revenging" trader and was constantly in the market, buying and selling, trying to get even, trying to get ahead. John was a "masked" investor, competitive and careful, feeling only as competent as his most recent trade. Steve traded small-cap stocks, and John traded the smaller size silver contracts.

One morning, during a general sales staff meeting, another employee commented that the Federal Reserve had just lowered the discount rate. Steve and John both exclaimed, "You're kidding!" much to the chagrin of their boss. They looked at each other with a knowing, conspiratorial look. After the meeting, Steve and John got together to discuss the market, and they have been good friends ever since. Steve helps John to settle down and avoid being the market's slave—he has taught John how to take half-profits when he's ahead of the game and how to avoid giving his gains back to the market. John has taught Steve how to look at the big picture with respect to winning and losing trades—he taught him to examine his performance over a longer period of time, rather than to measure his success on a trade-by-trade basis. John became a less passionate but more successful stock trader, and Steve became a more even-keeled silver trader. They shared strategy, techniques, and even enjoyed a more profitable relationship on the job as well.

You won't have to look far to find many co-workers who are also investors or traders. Don't overlook a golden opportunity to tap a helpful source that's just down the hall or at the next desk.

Bosses and Employees

Having your boss on your side can be a very profitable situation with respect to your job. But it can also be profitable with respect to your trading. Although many find it difficult to let their boss in on their trading and investing plans, the perspectives of a superior can be enlightening.

Most people keep their trading a secret from their boss because they don't want to divulge that they have another way of making money. Some fear that the boss will view them as too aggressive or greedy. Some worry that the boss will disparage their trading strategies.

Many of you might also feel that your investments are private business and not part of your professional life. However, if your boss trades, this attitude might cause you to miss out on a great learning opportunity. The nature of the relationship between an employee and a supervisor/boss is based on the exchange of information and experience. You learn all the aspects of your job and your responsibilities from him or her. Why not learn about new or more effective trading techniques as well? At the same time, you have found a common interest outside the job that can help to foster a more well-rounded, congenial relationship with your boss. There is, at any workplace, an informal social network, and the boss is an integral part of it. Sharing information about trading and investing often leads to better relationships, both professional and personal.

Case Study

Beverly

Beverly is a 60-year-old widow, whose husband left her with a sizable life insurance policy. She also inherited his passion for the futures market. Although he had only traded part-time, he was quite successful at calling turns in the bond market. Over the years, Beverly had learned a great deal about interest rates, inflation, unemployment statistics, and how these factors affected the price of bonds.

Beverly took the death of her husband quite hard. While she had always been somewhat shy and reserved, her husband's outgoing personality had always seemed to compensate for it, and they remained socially active over the years. Following his death, she kept to herself and had difficulty sleeping. She was deeply depressed, and her children were beginning to worry about her self-imposed isolation.

At the time of his death, Beverly's husband had a few open commodities positions. The idea of trading had always intrigued Beverly, and when she expressed this desire to her children, they encouraged her to give it a try. Beverly left the account open and kept $25,000 in it, but she couldn't get herself to take any new positions, even though she believed interest rates were going down and she could profit by going long bonds.

Beverly worked as a secretary in a group medical practice, and although she was shy, she also was pleasant to her colleagues. One day, one of the doctors came in and threw the morning newspaper down on the desk, lamenting that she had just lost $5000 in the stock market. Beverly began to tell the doctor about her husband's trades and her own thoughts on the bond market. The doctor, whose name was Jean, suggested that they discuss the market further and invited her to lunch. Beverly could tell that Jean listened closely to her opinions, and they began to meet regularly for lunch once a week.

Jean, who was conflicted about her stock market activity, would ask Beverly about her husband's trading techniques. She was also interested in Beverly's thoughts and opinions. Talking to Jean gave Beverly the energy and confidence to start trading—she did quite well, using not only her late husband's techniques but ones she formulated on her own. Beverly had found a sounding board in her boss, and her boss in turn appreciated Beverly's information. When the group was looking for an office manager, Jean suggested Beverly for the job, and she moved up into the position. Breaking down the boss/employee barrier and sharing a common interest outside the office proved helpful to both of them.

When to Use People at Work

- You discover that a boss, co-worker, or subordinate shares a common investing/trading interest.
- You've worked for a long time with someone who is perceptive about how you act in certain situations (under deadline, when there's a crisis, when you're put in charge of a project) and who might be able to translate that knowledge to an investing scenario.

- You have a special boss: This person has assisted you with serious problems before, and you believe he or she will help you resolve the mind/money difficulties you're experiencing.

MENTORS AND ROLE MODELS

Interestingly enough in the case of Jean and Beverly, both women served as role models for each other, even though their situations and backgrounds were very different. Remember, the key function of a role model is to help someone get past the internal obstacles to successful investing. This function was listed frequently in our surveys.

With the exception of the "paranoid" investor, successful part-time investors try to emulate someone, whether it's Warren Buffet, Jess Livermore, or Grahm and Dodd. Some model themselves after personal or family role models. What is important to remember is that finding someone to help you in your investing does not mean that you are dependent on their opinion or advice. It means that they are available to you for consultation. While you should take their advice and opinions into consideration, keep in mind that it is up to you to make your own decisions.

Of course, that's why overly cautious or "paranoid" investors have trouble with mentors. They become too dependent on their idols and heroes. This can also be true of the "masked" investor, who is plagued by self-esteem issues. The investor who hopes for a guru to step in and take over—someone to take all the risk and accept all the consequences, thereby releasing the investor of responsibility—is going to be disappointed.

But how do you find a mentor? For this type of relationship to work effectively, you should keep several things in mind. And remember, "it takes two to tango": A mentor has to be in the market for an investor-student, consciously or not.

1. There has to be common ground between a mentor and the student—love of the stock market, reverence for the history of Wall Street, devotion to a concept (like cycles, etc.)—even though almost everything else between the two may be very different.

2. The student must respect the mentor for more than just his or her experience in the market. And the mentor must respect the student for more than just his or her enthusiasm and willingness to learn.

3. Both parties must gain something from the relationship.

Obviously, if your role model is indirect—a historical figure or an authority or expert you have little chance of befriending—these rules will not apply.

You might say that the "mentor" is sort of the perfect mother/father figure for investing. A mentor is wise and helpful; has experience; cautions you when you are in danger; gives you ideas but doesn't force them on you; shares with you past successes and failures; and most importantly, listens to and respects you while accompanying you on your travels throughout your financial life.

When to Use a Mentor/Role Model

- You find yourself doubting your investing instincts, often with just cause (after a series of losses, for instance). You're certain that if you continue investing without an expert's help, you're going to continue to lose.

- You're in any cluster but the paranoid one.

- You read, hear about, or meet someone whose investing/trading ideas strike a positive chord. For whatever reason, that person's market advice is like a light in the darkness. Just as important, his or her ideas seem psychologically appropriate—they appeal not only to your pocketbook but to your mind.

CHAPTER 7

Dreams and Fantasies: Keys to Instinctive Trading

How do you use your dreams and fantasies as investing tools?

By paying attention to what they tell you about your "instincts." They reveal your "gut response" to a trade or investment—a response you should learn to trust. In Chapter 9 "The Conflicted Investor," we will discuss how dreams are the royal road to the unconscious. Let's figure out how to travel that road and read the signs along the way that tell us whether to buy or sell.

ENHANCING DREAM RECALL

The funny thing about dreams is that, no matter how engaging or vivid they may be, many of them are lost to us once we wake. On the average, we remember only a small percentage of our dreams.

But with practice and training, you can enhance your ability to recall dreams with greater accuracy and detail. One easy way to train yourself to remember is as follows:

When you wake, recall with as much detail as possible the circumstances and events of your dreams of the night before. Recall the sequence of events and repeat them out loud or write them down. You can keep our mind/money journal or a notebook by the bed for this activity. However, don't waste this time by trying to analyze or second-guess the meaning of your dreams. That can come later.

The same is true for daydreams. These waking fantasies can be equally helpful to you, because they are fueled by the same forces that spin your nocturnal fantasies. Interestingly enough, most people do not realize how many daydreams fill their waking hours. But, with practice, you should become adept at monitoring them. Record them in your journal as well.

SORTING THROUGH DREAM DETAILS

In the real world, a bombardment of information can be overwhelming. Do you have to know what the Australian dollar is doing? Is it imperative that you know all the details of a general strike in South Africa if you aren't involved in the precious metals market? Unless you trade currencies themselves, or gold/silver/platinum, the answer may be "no." Yet it may be important to keep up with the events surrounding the dollar, yen, and mark most of the time. In other words, with a ton of information coming at you, you are continually faced with decisions on what is and what is not important to you. The same is true for dreams—you have to separate the wheat from the chaff.

GET THE PLOT

Reduce your dreams and fantasies to their plots. For example, you may have a colorful dream of a circus, filled with many people and animals, teeming with events and actions, danger and excitement. That same dream may center on a small boy watching all this action, who then leaves to go outside and stand alone. The focus should be on him, rather than on the actors and clowns and high-wire acts. The hidden meaning lies with him and his motivation, purpose, and emotions.

You should look back on your dream and ask the following questions:

- Who's the star of the dream?
- What's the most important thing that took place during the dream?
- What seems merely descriptive or tangential to the important development?

Asking these questions gets you into the plot. In the plot, you'll find your instincts—instincts that are critical to investment decisions. The following example will show you just how critical they can be.

Case Study

Stan N.'s Three Dreams

A 51-year-old, divorced broker at a major brokerage house, Stan N. doesn't process trades for customers; at this point in his career he is responsible for the supervision of eight other brokers under him. He has a few clients of his own left over from the old days, but their accounts are fairly inactive. Stan does trade for his own account. He follows 6 to 9 small cap stocks and knows their trading range history well. He also keeps abreast of what's happening with the fundamentals of the companies themselves.

Stan has had a reasonable amount of success with his trading, and he has taken time to learn about himself as well. Through psychotherapy during his divorce and through self-tests, he has come to see that he is an overly cautious and, at times, a "paranoid" investor. It's tough for him to trust others, and he sometimes has difficulty trusting his own instincts. He has done well by exerting a fair degree of discipline over his trading system, through the use of support and resistance levels, and by carefully following the same trading stocks over a long period of time.

About four days ago, one of Stan's stocks broke through resistance on huge volume—about sevenfold its normal daily volume. The stock, a small electronics manufacturing company, had made no new announcements and Stan knew of no overwhelming fundamental news that would be coming out to justify such a move. The stock went from a price of 8 to 11 on that first day. On the next day, the price went from 11 to 12.5 on four times the normal volume. Stan knew that technically this was significant, but he wasn't wild about chasing the stock. A technically talented and astute broker outside Stan's group was discussing the stock at lunch and advised the other brokers to buy, declaring a move like this was significant and portended a much higher price in the future. Stan was perplexed about what he should do—he didn't want to rush into anything. During this time, he had a series of three dreams:

> *Dream 1.* Four dogs are standing behind a fence eating, but they don't like being caged in. Four other dogs run by, and it seems as if the two packs are about to bark at each other. Instead, the four dogs who are inside start trying to jump over the fence to join those on the outside.

Dream 2. A little girl is licking an ice-cream cone while sitting on a bench in a park. Stan is walking by and notices her, thinking to himself that an ice-cream cone would taste good to him right now. He starts to think of the nearest ice-cream store. The little girl offers him a lick of her cone. He is reluctant to take it because he is wary of what others might think—"taking candy from a baby," and so on. He actually would love to take a lick and give the cone back to her, but he is worried about how it would look.

Dream 3. An old man and a young man are lying in the shade on a patch of grass near a sandy beach. The younger man has a transistor radio, tuned to their favorite classical music station. The old man looks like Stan's father. Suddenly, there is a thunderstorm, and the transistor radio turns to static, mixing all the channels. It is raining everywhere, except for the small patch of grass on which they lay. They are worried that it is going to start pouring down on them as well. In an instant, an incredible piece of classical music begins to play on the radio, unlike anything that either of them have heard before. It is absolutely beautiful and flawless, and they are completely mesmerized by the song. Then, the young man realizes with a start that he must get to work by 4:00 PM or he could lose his job.

What Stan's Dreams Mean

Stan keeps a mind/money journal, and while reviewing his notes about these dreams, he first extracts the plots. For Dream 1, he writes: "This is a dream about eight animals who look as if they are going to fight with one another, but end up wanting to be together. They want to run free, but four of them are fenced in."

For Dream 2, he writes: "I see a younger person with something I want. She offers it to me, but I am hesitant to accept it for fear that I will be accused of taking advantage of her."

For Dream 3, he writes: "A father and son are listening to music they both enjoy. Outside events threaten to destroy their common activity, but actually result in an even more wonderful and totally unsuspected gain. The son then realizes that he has to act and cannot allow himself to get lulled into forgetting about the time."

Stan's Conclusions

From his knowledge of his own psychological obstacles to successful investing, Stan realizes that he has always done better without a mentor and that following his own systems provides him with the most success. At times, he is plagued with uncertainty, not knowing where his instincts are taking him. He rarely takes the suggestions of others too seriously and has done well following his own hunches.

The dream helps Stan accept that the other brokers he works with should not be viewed with suspicion— they share Stan's goals. He acknowledges that the eight dogs in his dream represent the eight brokers with whom he lunches. The dogs remind him of the word's negative investing connotation; in the past, he had thought of the electronics company stock as being a "dog." The brokers and the stock were fused together in the form of the dogs; the stock was breaking free, while Stan still felt he was fenced in.

In regard to the second dream, Stan concludes that taking ice cream from the child is related to his accepting the technical advice of the younger stockbroker. He knows enough about technical trading to realize that this might be a significant move with more to come, but he is reluctant to invest heavily in the stock at this point for fear that others will think he stole the ideas of the younger man. Rationally, Stan realizes that no one would really think that about him or any of the others if they were to go long. Stan decides that this dream is about how it is hard for him to accept the gift of permission from the younger broker.

Interpreting the third dream, Stan decides that it is about him and his father, and it is centered around his overly cautious tendencies. He never could enjoy these kinds of common activities with his dad. If he were to go ahead with the stock buy, he would have the pleasure of sharing this common breakout with a younger man himself. As the son in the dream, he knew it had to do with "acting" so that it would not be too late.

Stan waited for the stock to take a breather and back off its recent gains. When it did, he went long with a large position. From time to time, he would chat with the younger broker on the technical status of the stock as it continued to grow, although slowly, in price and volume.

Stan's dreams helped him overcome the obstacles caused by his paranoia. He acted appropriately and, in fact, enjoyed sharing the risk and strategy of the younger technical trader during the time when they were both long on the electronics stock.

FOCUS ON THE MAIN EMOTION

Once you have identified the plot or plots of your dreams, pay close attention to the emotions they engender. Emotion gives you motive. Thus, the major feelings in any given dream serve as the key to its meaning.

Looking at Stan's dreams, you can see that fear (of the fight with the four dogs) is the first emotion that plays in Dream 1, but it is quickly followed by hope (the hope of getting out from behind the fence).

In Dream 2, Stan records three main emotions. The first emotion is envy: He envies the young girl with the ice cream. The second emotion is guilt: He is tempted to take something from a younger person. The third emotion is fear: He is afraid he will be falsely accused of wrongdoing. Also present is a fragment of appreciation, which occurs when she offers him the cone, but it is quickly overshadowed by the fear.

In Dream 3, Stan recorded that his main feelings were contentment (listening to music with a father figure), fear (of the thunderstorm), joy (at hearing such beautiful music), and anxiety (about being late to work).

To interpret these emotions in a practical way, let's separate them from the dreams.

APPLY THE EMOTIONS TO TRADING

The prominent emotions represented in Stan's dreams are fear, hope, envy, contentment, joy, and anxiety. We can apply each of these emotions to his trading situation.

Stan fears that he is being led astray by the younger technician. He is also afraid of chasing the stock price. Hope applies to the breakout and the promise of a very large return. Contentment may relate to his having followed this stock for some time and knowing its movement. Joy may be something that he is holding back. He feels anxiety about not jumping on the bandwagon immediately.

The sum total of these emotions demonstrates to Stan that taking a significant position in the stock is wise. He scrutinizes each emotion in relation to the specific investment decision, and his scrutiny yields the same message: Buy! The emotions reveal Stan's instincts, and his instincts are all pushing him toward the stock.

Isolate your emotions as Stan did. Summarize them with a word, and then overlay that word on an investment/trading decision that's occupying your mind. If the word is fear and the decision is whether to invest in a highly risky project, you might think twice before taking the plunge. If another emotional word isolated from the dreams is panic, and that's exactly what the prospect of investing in this project raises inside you, then the investment may well be wrong for you. At the very least, it goes against your grain, your gut.

DAYDREAMS AND NIGHTDREAMS

This same technique is useful when applied to your daydreams. Daydreams are easier to capture and remember. For example, let's analyze the daydreams of Scott, a pharmacist who sometimes dabbles in the OEX market.

Case Study

Scott's Daydreams

The stock market has been in a trading range for about six months, but the volume is poor. Scott has been making some money by going long at support and shorting near the top. Commissions, however, are eating away most of his profit. The market hits support and actually breaks through, slightly to the downside. Then it recovers. Upside momentum and breadth are once again meager. Scott finds himself in the trading range again. This whole process is wearing on him—he feels eroded by it.

Scott's work as a pharmacist provides him with a decent living. His business is not great but he enjoys it, and he often has time to follow the markets closely. Scott feels somewhat tired and depressed; recently, he has lost enthusiasm for his trading and can concentrate only when he makes an extreme effort.

One day, during his drive to work, Scott begins daydreaming. He pictures an ordinary living room, and in front of the picture window sits a vase full of roses that won't open into full bloom. Suddenly, a ball comes crashing through the window and smashes the vase. In his daydream, Scott is very startled.

Later that day, after finishing inventory, Scott sits down at his desk with plans to chart out the market's numbers for the day. A bus drives by, leaving a huge black cloud of exhaust that lingers in the air outside. Scott wanders off into another daydream and imagines himself running after the bus. He is really angry at the driver and jumps on board to confront him. The bus driver gets up, rips the coin meter from the floor, and throws it at him. Scott ducks, and the meter smashes through the glass door of the bus. The glass fragments seem so sharp that they could cut someone, leaving the person to bleed to death. In this daydream, Scott is not afraid but feels confusion at the driver, who has now calmly sat down. In a way, Scott feels like a spectator of the entire episode.

Scott begins to look for the meaning behind his vivid daydreams. He had been planning to go long when the market neared support. He had been in the market, both ways, during the past six months. The emotions of his daydreams reflect frustration (the roses will not bloom), surprise (breaking glass vase and bus door), and anger (at the smoke outside).

After a careful examination of these daydreams, Scott decides to take a break from the market. He has been semidepressed and unenthusiastic about his trades anyway. He realizes that he is angry at the market for not moving and that he would be very surprised if a move one way or the other would break through the barriers. Rather than riding the market up and down, Scott decides to wait for a breakout. Having reached this decision, he feels pleased at pulling out, rather than remaining paralyzed by the eroding market and support.

Two weeks later, the market broke down through support decisively and dropped three hundred points on strong durable goods orders and signs that inflation was coming on strong. Lots of money managers dumped stocks. When the market hit a very solid floor around the 200-day moving average, Scott moved back in.

FINDING COMMON DREAM ELEMENTS

As you can see from the examples of Stan and Scott's dreams, paying attention to the plot and emotions of dreams and fantasies can give you an edge on your own inner trading mentality. Analyze your dreams by looking for similarities in them. The glass vase, the glass doors, breaking of objects, and the feeling of surprise were common elements of Scott's fantasies. When examining your dreams and fantasies, look for a common theme in the following four areas:

1. *Action.* Hitting, breaking, running, paying.
2. *Setting.* Buses, living rooms, beaches, yards.
3. *Actors/Actresses.* Parents, children, dogs, drivers.
4. *Props.* Vases, radios, glass doors, fences.

Apply the common elements you identify to your current trading life. Look for the glass barriers—figure out who or what you are angry at.

USING FREE ASSOCIATION

Remember the dogs in Stan's first dream? Stan felt that the caged dogs represented himself. He spontaneously "free associated" himself with the unique element of the characters in his dream. Through further examination, Stan was able to relate the dogs to his stock as well. What came to mind during his analysis was that "every dog has its day"—an old Wall Street saying about unexciting stocks moving at one time or another.

Stan employed free association to his second dream as well. Remember the ice-cream cone? He thought to himself that he would be "taking candy from a baby," and it led to his worry about taking the young trader's advice about the breakout of his stock.

When you notice "out-of-place" colors, items, actions, or people in a dream or fantasy, let yourself think about the visions and relationships that come into mind—look for any possible connections to your current situation. This kind of free association has the potential to help you make profitable decisions.

To help you "free associate," here are some questions to ask yourself regarding the out-of-place elements:

- Do the elements suggest a cliché or saying to you?
- What possible significance could the elements have in your investing/trading life?
- Do you feel the elements are positive or negative; do they suggest buy or sell; do they signify risk or safety?

STEP-BY-STEP DREAM ANALYSIS

Don't let dreams go unnoticed. Remember Carl Jung's famous saying that "a dream unanalyzed is like a letter unopened." Follow these steps:

1. Write down your dreams, fantasies, and daydreams.

2. Extract their plots.

3. Isolate the prominent emotions.

4. Look for common elements.

5. Free associate to out-of-place features.

6. Apply everything to your investing or trading situation.

No, this isn't a simple, scientific process. You'll need to use your imagination. In a way, it's a challenging game. We're asking you to treat your dreams as clues to solve the mystery of the investing/trading process.

Remember, this isn't your only tool: To rely solely on your dreams as your investment advisor is the same as depending on only one piece of market data before making a buy-or-sell decision.

Dreams are useful only within the context of your other tools and your knowledge of the psychological cluster or clusters that apply to you. Your dreams and fantasies, interpreted along the lines we suggest, may help you identify how you really feel about a particular trade or investment. And how you really feel—as opposed to how you think you feel—should point you toward the right investing move.

Perhaps you can best use your dreams as tiebreakers. When you're torn between alternatives, when you can't decide whether to buy or sell, whether to invest in stocks or bonds, whether to listen to Guru A or Guru B, look to your dreams. Toss them up as you would a coin and see how they land. If you follow the six steps outlined in this chapter, it doesn't matter if it's heads or tails—you've greatly increased the odds that you'll win no matter how the coin lands.

CHAPTER 8

How to "Lose Your Mind"

James Joyce, a famous poet and writer, sought the advice of the equally famous psychiatrist, Dr. Carl Jung. Joyce, whose work is admired for its startling and often bizarre wordplay, consulted with Jung about his daughter, who had schizophrenia. Joyce was desperate to understand why his daughter's incoherent ramblings were so similar to the phrasing of his prose and poetry, and yet she had been diagnosed as a schizophrenic, while he was thought to be brilliant.

To the writer's questions, Jung replied:

The difference is that she falls, whereas you dive.

As you'll see, a conscious decision to explore a foreign inner world differs greatly from an unconscious one. Intentional behavior that allows you to escape the humdrum prison of your daily routine can be highly beneficial; it can give you the breathing space necessary to help your mind reassert control over your money.

"VACATING" THE REAL WORLD

It should come as no surprise that one of the most useful tools that professional traders and money managers employ to overcome psychological obstacles is that of "getting away from it all." They simply take vacations. The concept sounds so simple and so obvious that it shouldn't even warrant discussion. But as Voltaire once said: "Common sense isn't so common."

One of the greatest tools you have available is the ability to "send your mind away." You can be sitting on the subway, driving downtown in your car, or tied up in a boring business meeting—but not really be there at all. You can be thinking of an argument you had with your spouse last night and be transported back to your living room, even as you are sitting in that staff meeting. You can be fantasizing about an upcoming vacation to Maui, even as you are really at home in front of your computer, watching the daily market reports. You can be daydreaming about piloting the space shuttle, while in reality you are riding the elevator up to your boss's office. We are able to use this precious freedom of the mind, most often unconsciously, to "vacate" our current circumstances, especially when they are less than ideal or engaging.

TAKING A BREAK VERSUS SUFFERING A BREAKDOWN

Psychiatrists have known for a long time that many severely ill patients lack the ability to vacate in this fashion. They are often locked into reality in a terrifying way. They have lost that freedom to transport themselves into a distant daydream and cannot lose themselves mentally. When they can no longer take it, they break—they don't take a break. Their minds take off, leaving them behind. They have lost their minds and can't find them anymore.

Our psychological investing and trading types suffer from a milder malady. Although they are not prisoners of the here and now in such an extreme form as is a psychotic, they are still in great need of "vacating." Consumed and conflicted investors can't seem to "give it up." They feel they have to be in the market at all times, and they are constantly worrying, planning, watching.

To a certain extent, this is true of the paranoid trader as well. Paranoid traders can't seem to relax; they are always wary of what might happen next, and who may be out to get them.

But this problem can affect almost every type of trader or investor. It is very, very easy to find yourself consumed and obsessed with money—in many ways, our society sanctions these obsessions.

Learning how to vacate and to take a break, therefore, is an essential lesson for most traders and investors. Breaks can last a few minutes to a few weeks. The important thing is to take them. The following list describes a few kinds of breaks. For maximum benefit, you should incorporate a variety of them into your routine.

1. *Pacing.* During ongoing activities, such as day trading, you must learn how to pace yourself. This means alternating between periods of intense activity and periods of markedly decreased activity, requiring little of your attention span. These "pauses" should occur when you do not have to respond quickly to a current market flux. This is hard advice to follow for certain types of investors—paranoid, obsessive, and others. They refuse to allow themselves a break, sometimes on the theory that if they stop, they'll give someone else an opportunity to gain on them. But you can't go all out every minute of every day. Even the greatest professional athletes pace themselves during games or races, gathering their strength for when they'll most need it. You, too, should find a pace that suits you.

2. *Mental Stops.* "Mental stops" are the equivalent of a conventional coffee break. Four to six times a day, you

should be taking a mental stop—taking your mind out of gear and allowing it to idle. Whether you close your eyes, do a transcendental mantra, or simply chat with someone on the phone is not important. That you "take five," however, is essential.

3. *Days Off.* You should regularly plan for some days off, at least one a month. This forces you physically to vacate your workplace and trading/investing activities. Do something different—alone or with someone else. Use this time to refresh yourself. It will allow you to come back with a clear head and reduce the psychological pressure you are under. Even if you are a fussy investor, you can "unstick" yourself with an occasional day off.

4. *Taking Real Vacations.* Sometimes, you need to leave the scene of your psychological crimes. You should physically remove yourself from the drumbeat of conflict, revenge, shame and humiliation, fatigue, obsession, and fear. Two or three weeks away from the markets each year can provide you with a much-needed perspective when you return to trading.

Case Study

Janet L. and "The Big Picture"

Janet L. was a fussy, part-time trader. She had discovered both the stock and the stock option markets while working as the regional manager of a large, expensive retail chain of specialty department stores, shortly after receiving her MBA. She followed gold and silver and traded their options. She had been told that Larry Williams's book on how he made a million dollars in commodities provided an excellent timing tool, so she studied it intensely and then set about the business of timing her option trades. She precisely pinpointed the trading cycle of several futures contracts and learned how to tell if they should be bottoming or topping. She kept her charts and data columns religiously. She expected complete and perfect executions from her broker, and he satisfied her most of the time.

At home, Janet would sit at her desk for hours, examining her charts and numbers. Her friends would tease her for being such a "busy bee," accusing her of "buzzing" all the time. At times, she wouldn't even get up to eat until she finished graphing that last set of numbers. Although she insisted on completeness, she would often lose sight of the big picture.

She would get her futures charts right but often would forget to take the larger market into account. She'd get her orders right but didn't pay attention to the overall topping processes. She'd be correct in being long futures, but when the overall market went down, she found herself unable to capitalize on the new trend.

Janet decided to ask her friend Cynthia for advice. Cynthia, a former futures broker, was 15 years older than Janet; they had met in the same MBA program. Cynthia was a proponent of the "relaxation response"—a technique for relaxation whereby you spend 10 minutes twice daily clearing the mind while repeating some kind of a hymn, prayer, phrase, or mantra. If worries or thoughts should come into your mind during this period, you are to let them "pass through" while you return to a calm, clear mind-set. Cynthia suggested that Janet do at least one of these 10-minute sessions in the middle of her evening charting to "clear her head." Janet tried it, and it helped her improve her perspective of how her actions related to the "big picture."

GETTING DISTRACTED—ON PURPOSE

Going to the movies, watching television, reading books or magazines—these are all common forms of what we call "distraction." Much press has been given to the addiction that we have developed to television, video games, and other alleged mindless pursuits. We agree that, in excess, this type of behavior can be detrimental. Yet, this notion of "getting mindless" is an important aid in clearing out the investing cobwebs.

The ability to vacate, or take breaks, is the key difference between having your "mind over money" versus having "money over your mind." When money rules the mind, you no longer have control. You lose perspective. Your ability to differentiate a good trade from a bad one diminishes; you've lost your natural skill to take a step back and analyze a situation from an objective distance. Without any breaks, you resemble someone who refuses to sleep—you become groggy and fuzzy-headed, losing your decision-making edge.

That is why scheduling time away from the constant struggle to make money is so important. You must schedule some "playtime" for yourself. Keep track of the time spent at play: Make sure you take a moderate amount. In this way, you are able to take control of your actions, at least in the sense that you determine when you're going to try to make money and when you're going to do something else. Think of it as a regulated way of "losing your mind." To paraphrase Jung, rather than take a fall, take a dive!

INVESTOR TYPES, PLAY TYPES

You should structure your playtime according to your psychological type. What works for the masked investor may prove useless for the fussy one. Take a break with the following in mind:

- *Conflicted.* Movies may be an excellent outlet for this type of investor. Movie after movie portrays human conflicts, and in a highly visceral manner. These films may provide an unconscious outlet for relieving the inner grind that plagues you. Just seeing your conflict mirrored on a screen can be an escape valve for all the pressure of conflict that's been building up inside you.

- *Consumed.* Sporting events are often beneficial. The passion of the win–lose situation may put competition in perspective. You might find yourself less concerned about winning at any cost. For a while at least, you won't be consumed by your own passions but will enter into the passions of those engaging in a particular spectator sport. If you eat, drink, and sleep index futures, it may be a blessed respite from what's consuming you to watch Michael Jordan soar to the basket with a similar single-minded passion.

- *Masked.* Relief is provided by reading *People Magazine* and biographies of other people, or by watching television shows such as *Lifestyles of the Rich and Famous.* By immersing yourself in the masks of others, you lose the need to conceal your own true self. In addition, the masked investor can benefit from performing altruistic tasks, such as working in a shelter or volunteering for a charity. Doing good deeds of this nature may boost your self-confidence and self-esteem while, at the same time, such activities decrease your need for a quick-fix success in the market. Always remember that you should spend this time doing something that you enjoy. Don't play at something that feels like work to you—let it be fun.

- *Fussy.* A trip to the racetrack or comparison shopping may do the trick. For the fussy investor who is much concerned with order and detail, playtime activities that require "fun" immersions in various numbers (horseracing odds, prices) can provide satisfaction if you crave the concrete (rather than the abstract). If you get your neatness fix during playtime, you may not need it as much during your investing.

- *Paranoid.* Plan trips to nearby places where you're sure you won't run into anyone you know. The key is to do something enjoyable without worrying that others are judging you based on past experience or preconceptions. A dinner at an out-of-the-way restaurant or a bicycle ride miles removed from your neighborhood might work.

- *Depressed.* Try distracting yourself with tales of sex or aggression—be it through movies, books, or television. You need vicarious excitement and adventure to provide the proper distraction.

REST, NAPS, AND SLEEP

When employing the technique of losing your mind, remember the comment of world-class spy Jason Bourne, a character of the novelist Robert Ludlum: "Rest is a Weapon."

Make sure that you keep a healthy supply of this weapon in your arsenal. Without proper rest, the mind will be much more susceptible to the negative effects of your psychological type: If you're paranoid, for instance, you'll be even more paranoid if you're not well rested. You'll probably mistake a small dip in the market as the Second Coming of the Crash. Resting can mean taking a break, lying down for a brief nap, getting a good night's sleep, or choosing one of many other restful "activities."

Taking naps is not just for kids. Rest is the root of the term "restorative"—and restoring yourself should be your goal. Pardon the pun, but you can rest assured that forcing yourself to take a nap requires a great deal of commitment and discipline. Finding, and justifying, the time for a nap can be difficult. You may have to overcome a lot of internal embarrassment, self-criticism, and fear that someone will discover you're napping and think you are weak or lazy. But that should not deter you. Napping has many benefits—physically, mentally, and emotionally.

A half-hour nap can have a remarkable impact on mood, energy level, and the ability to think quickly. It is well known that the "biological clock" works on 90-minute cycles, so it is natural to feel tired and sleepy at some point in the morning and in the afternoon. Similar cycles can be seen in normal nighttime sleep. When you don't get enough sleep during the night, taking a nap can significantly boost your performance—not only in your trading, but in almost every other aspect of your life.

The same can be said of nighttime sleep. Getting enough sleep every night is crucial to your performance. Chronic sleep deprivation can diminish your ability to overcome the psychological obstacles to your investing or trading, so make sure you do your best to get enough rest. One of our professional survey respondents was emphatic about the impact of sleep on his mood and, subsequently, on his trading performance. When he was unable to get a good night's rest, he found himself tired, depressed, and unable to think clearly. But with a full eight hours, he was energetic, enthusiastic, and eager to hit the floor.

Investing and trading, more than many other activities, require energy and a clear mind. You need to be alert to subtle market movements, absorbing and processing large amounts of information and making decisions on the turn of a dime. If you're sleep deprived, you can do none of these things well. Many investors who make psychologically based mistakes could avoid them with a bit more sleep.

Of all of the tools we're offering you, this one is the easiest to use, so don't ignore it just because it seems too easy or obvious.

TROUBLE SIGNS OF AN OVERWORKED MIND

It's not always easy to know when to employ the "losing your mind" technique. Many people we've talked to who should have used it didn't: They honestly didn't think they needed to give their minds any time off.

Many of our psychological types eschew time off. They're too tough to admit that they need a vacation or more sleep; or they're so fearful of what may happen when they take a break (I'll miss the best trade of my life") that they can't shut down.

Consider the following signs. They're indicative of people who need to lose their minds for a bit—for just enough time to regain the perspective, energy, and mental acuity they may have temporarily lost.

- *You've Overlooked Crucial Information.* You forget to factor in a critical piece of trading/investing knowledge. You can't understand how you could have overlooked this information—it's not like you to ignore the rumors of that Fortune 500 company's layoff and buy stock in the company.

- *You're Walking Around in a Haze.* It's as if a mist has descended. You try to do some simple calculations necessary for an investment and you just can't get your mind around it. You try to analyze a chart and you can't get a clear picture of a trend.

- *Everything Has to Do with Money.* You see a beautiful sunset and it triggers thoughts of a declining market; you start to eat a pork chop and can't take another bite until you've debated whether you should go long on pork bellies; you go fishing but your thoughts are on what lies beneath the surface of a report just issued by a company you have your eye on.

- *You Don't Have Time for Friends or Family.* Looking back, you realize that you haven't seen your close group of friends in months; that you haven't taken your kid to a ballgame or your wife out to dinner; that you haven't seen any of the movies nominated for an Academy Award (and you love movies). All your spare time has been spent on investing/trading.

- *Time Off Scares You.* Perhaps your wife insists that you accompany her on a trip to Bermuda; or you find yourself roped into jury duty. It might be nothing more than having to take a few days off to attend a wedding. Whatever it is, you dread the prospect of time off. The idea of decreasing the amount of time you trade/invest by even a minute is highly distasteful.

If these signs sound familiar, consider some of the losing-your-mind options in this chapter. Whatever you lose in time, you'll more than make up for in sounder investments and trades.

Now, let's see how you can adapt this tool and those of the preceding chapters to suit your psychological type. The following chapters will examine each of the six types in depth, enabling you to determine if you fall in a given category, what you can do about it to positively influence your investing success, and how others like you have coped. Though you might already think you know your type—either instinctively or through the information provided in earlier chapters—keep an open mind. For one thing, you may be a combination of types: It's not unusual for traders and investors to possess characteristics of two or even three of our clusters. Also, it's easy to make mistakes when you are trying to assess your type—it is much easier for you to fool yourself than to fool others. Chapters 9 through 14 (and Chapter 15, which discusses "wild card" types) will help you avoid those mistakes and enable you to figure out an "action plan" based on your particular psychological makeup.

CHAPTER 9

The Conflicted Investor

Our survey revealed that out of all the investor profiles, the conflicted profile is the most common and has the most negative impact on investing performance. Though the types of conflicts that affect our respondents vary greatly, the net effect may be investing/trading losses.

Because conflict is such a common mind-over-money problem—and because the conflict is often subtle—it's a particularly dangerous trap for investors. You may not have a conflict between investing in stocks versus bonds, but that doesn't mean you're not conflicted. The vast majority of our conflicted respondents didn't tell us they were conflicted; they didn't write, "I find myself missing out on winning trades because I have a deep-seated guilt about making money."

Most people don't think about investing that way. But they drop hints that give away their conflict, often feeling relieved after losses. They go back and forth on the trades they make—they are terribly inconsistent. They may be competitive as well, always in the market, hoping to beat it; and yet, a successful trade or investment may cause them anxiety. Inevitably, conflicted investors are not successful investors.

Having talked with many conflicted investors over the years, we've heard a frequent complaint from them: "I always seem to get involved with brokers and investments that are bad for me."

Why? Are they masochists, forever being drawn to brokers who would make Ivan Boesky look like Mother Theresa? Or are they like the guy who's always hooking himself up with women who are bad for him; he knows the women will drive him crazy, but he can't help himself?

The right answer is the latter, of course. Conflict is like a spiderweb, and the investor is a fly, caught unexpectedly in its silken grasp.

If you can recognize the web—the conflict—for what it is, you can escape its negative impact on your investments. Yet how do you recognize conflict, or more to the point, your specific conflict?

"IT'S THE STORY OF MY LIFE"

Start with a theme. Try to write down a one-sentence theme, something personal, that illustrates a recurring problem in your past. For instance: "My mother would humiliate me and my father stood by and just watched." Or: "I would bring home my report card hoping to see my dad's face shine and he would say, 'Only a B?'"

These statements are theme songs for conflicted investors. An investor suffers a modest loss on a stock position and futilely waits for Dad to step in and stop the carnage ("my father stood by and just watched"). Or an investor profits from a gold option investment and instead of continuing this successful tactic embarks on a more risky course (he is thinking, "Only a B?").

Time and again, investors replay these themes. From a psychological perspective, they're slaves to repetition compulsion. Put more prosaically, they're gamblers betting against the house, placing bet after bet on the same unlucky number.

How do you get back on equal (or near-equal) footing with the house? By understanding the four components of conflict and their power. If you doubt their power, ask yourself why you got out of that real estate partnership just before it paid off or why you put all your money in a stock everyone told you was no good (they were right). You're not dumb or cursed. You're simply conflicted.

How are you conflicted? There are four possibilities. We can categorize them as follows: (1) wishes, (2) criticisms, (3) feelings, (4) defenses. Let's take a look at each of them.

YOUR WISH IS YOUR COMMAND

I wish to have a million dollars. I wish to be President. I wish to drive a Ferrari.

Sometimes you know what your wishes are and sometimes you don't. In either case, they're always present in conflicts.

You've all probably heard about the Oedipus complex: A boy wishes to best his father and win his rightful place with his mother. Translate that to an investment scenario: Your dad made a killing in the stock market and you want to make an even bigger killing in the commodities market. Or your father was a timid investor who wound up on skid row. You're going to do it differently, buying mutual funds and building a nest egg.

Remember, you're not investing in a vacuum. Many of you make investment decisions based on a hunch, a gut feeling, an instinct. Only it's more than that. It's a wish. A wish that might have been formed years ago and is rearing its unconscious head to flaw your investment logic.

THE VOICE OF CONSCIENCE

The second ingredient, criticism (or prohibition), is that little voice that strongly suggests you shouldn't do what you want. The voice is somewhat irritating; it's characterized by the shrill tone of the self-righteous. For instance, you say to yourself, "I want to go on a three-week vacation this year. I'm tired of going for only one week and never really unwinding."

Immediately, that little voice pipes up: "It costs too much money and besides, you don't have that much vacation time set aside. Don't be so indulgent and selfish."

Again, let's look at this voice from an investment perspective. All the information you've gathered tells you to take your money out of a mutual fund and put it into the stock of an emerging growth company in the high-tech sector. The mutual fund is a long-term investment; you're banking on it to fund your kids' college educations. But you've studied this new company; you're satisfied with its management, its marketing, its products. Everything you've read and heard tells you it's going to take off.

But just as you're dialing your broker's number to make the transfer, that little voice sneaks up on you and demands, "What are you doing! Can you be so short-sighted that you'd be willing to risk your children's future on some company that could be out of business within the year?"

Living with that little voice is like having a nightmarish mother-in-law in your house. It's always going to produce conflict.

THE MOTION OF EMOTION

All conflict is accompanied by feelings. You should be aware that those feelings—those emotions—aren't always neat and clean. The joy of victory doesn't necessarily mean 100 percent smiles, and the agony of defeat doesn't translate into total depression.

Remember that the conflicts derailing good judgment are often unconscious. That's why you shouldn't be surprised when your emotions don't mirror the events that produced them.

You've lost $10,000 in the stock market, yet you're whistling in the investor's graveyard; you feel a strange sense of relief. Or you've made $10,000, but you're oddly depressed.

Don't dismiss these "irrational" feelings. They have a cause, rooted in conflict. They're clues to what's going on.

"I HAVEN'T GOT TIME FOR THE PAIN"

Defense mechanisms are the fourth ingredient of conflict. They include rationalizations, externalizations (somebody else's fault), stoicism, denials, somatizations (getting back pains, headaches, etc.), constant jokes, and many others. We use defense mechanisms to keep pain at bay.

You get drunk because you can't figure how to extricate yourself from a perilous market position.

You have to make a major decision about an investment and develop a migraine that sends you to the doctor, which helps you postpone the decision.

You blame your investment losses on your broker even though they're the result of specific instructions you gave him.

Conflicted investors are quite imaginative in their defensive reactions. In fact, there are 10 common defensive reactions to conflict, and you should understand what each of them entails and determine if any of them apply to you.

THE TOP TEN CONFLICTED DEFENSES

1. *Denial.* You make a bad trade, lose money, and then pretend it never happened. You can't admit—to yourself or others—that you backed a slow-running nag.

2. *Distortion.* You'll acknowledge a loss, but you sugar-coat it. If someone asks you how you did on a trade that resulted in a sizable loss, you'll say, "Oh, I lost, but I didn't take a bad hit like a lot of other people."

3. *Projection.* You "project" the loss on to someone or something else. It was your broker's fault, an unexpected event in the marketplace, the stars weren't properly aligned.

4. *Fatigue.* You begin to feel like a wet noodle. You react to investing problems by mimicking the symptoms of some vague kind of disease. Rather than doing your investing homework and doubling your efforts to win, you cloak yourself in a cozy lethargy.

5. *Doing and Undoing.* Here, your defense is indecision. You get on the phone to your broker and say, "Place the order." Then you pause and say, "Wait, don't place the order." You vacillate between positions, between types of investments, between amounts of investments. You set out on one investing course, reverse it, then reverse it again.

6. *Masochism.* You react to a bad investment by saying, "Screw it, I might as well lose it all." You take pleasure in the pain of a stock downturn or market plunge. There's an almost perverse delight when your investment decisions turn out to be the wrong ones.

7. *Identification with the Aggressor.* This is a more subtle defense mechanism than the others. It's most apparent in people who get beat by the market but feel a strange sort of kinship with the market as it beats them. You identify with the powerful, inexorable forces of the marketplace, even if they hurt you. You respond in a similarly aggressive way, taking a swipe

at your dog or throwing an ashtray at your computer screen.

8. *Rationalization.* Here's a much more common defense mechanism. When you lose in the market, you say things like "Winning really isn't that important to me"; "This is just a hobby"; "You win some, you lose some."

9. *Altruism.* A cousin of rationalization, this defense tells you to forget your loss by helping someone or something else. You figure that an investment, even a losing one, will make your broker happy. Or you think that investing is good for the economy. Or that it's worthwhile to invest in a certain company.

10. *Humor.* It's not always healthy to laugh at a loss, especially when the joke's on you. After an investment goes sour, you chuckle and think, "Well, at least I still have my health, though I'd better steer clear of investments in that insurance company." Or you tell a friend, "Hey, I have a great way for you to get rich. Give me a list of ten stocks, I'll tell you the nine I like, and you invest in the tenth." You use humor as a shield.

These are all topical anaesthetics. They take care of the surface depression and irritation. Unfortunately, the real problems still exist and, if left untreated, can render you dysfunctional. They weaken your investment judgment. If you can identify them when they're in motion, then you can see your conflict at work. Once you spot your particular defense, you should be alert to an underlying conflict that's hurting your investing performance.

OEDIPUS ON WALL STREET—CYCLES OF AMBITION AND DEFEAT

We've covered the four ingredients of conflict: wishes, criticisms, feelings, and defenses. If you're uncertain if these ingredients pertain to you, there's another sign of a conflicted investor that you should be aware of: the zero-sum game. You win a little, you lose a little, and in the end you come out even. The only problem, of course, is that maintaining equilibrium is not the goal of investing. Why spend all your time, energy, and commission costs if you're not going to have any more money than when you started?

The answer—you're a victim of the Oedipus complex. As you may recall, Oedipus, unknowingly, is raised by people who aren't his real parents; he grows up and meets a man on a road who is his real father, only Oedipus doesn't know this. The man insults Oedipus, and out of pride (the fatal flaw), he kills his father. He journeys on, and later falls in love with the queen of the kingdom, who is Oedipus's mother (again, he doesn't realize this at the time). He marries her and becomes the king. Immediately, he tries to discover who killed the former king. When Oedipus learns that he killed his own father and has married his own mother, he blinds himself and exiles himself from the kingdom.

The zero-sum investor moves about blind and in exile. The relevance of the Oedipus complex for investors is what happens after successful investments. The "balancing" act performed by criticism and emotion is summed up by one word: guilt.

Now most of you won't admit to feeling guilty after a successful investment. How can you? The desire to be punished is nowhere near consciousness.

If you're like most people, you may read this and think to yourself, "Yeah, I just made $100,000 and boy do I feel guilty; I feel so bad that I'm going to punish myself by making another $100,000."

It's difficult to understand something you can't see. It's natural to be skeptical. But suspend your disbelief for a moment. You don't have to admit that you feel guilty about making money. Just give yourself the benefit of the doubt and accept that the Oedipal conflict in investors is real.

To put it in more real terms, think about investing relative to success. Everyone wants to be successful, right? On the surface, of course. But deeper down, the answer isn't so clear-cut, as shown in the following example:

Case Study

Madeline B.'s Success Anxiety

Madeline B. hated to lose. In high school, she was ranked sixth in a class of 1200 students. She was a cheerleader, served as president of a number of clubs, and was invited to the prom by one of the school's most popular boys. Madeline could have been the class valedictorian if she had applied herself in two difficult courses her senior year, but she slacked off a bit—something about being the number one student in the class bothered her. She applied to a number of prestigious colleges, and though she was rejected by Radcliffe and Yale (she told her friends that she thought she blew the interviews, and she was right), she was accepted by Princeton and went there, majoring in economics.

Madeline considered herself to be a "good" person. She was ethical, disciplined, and generous. She was also very judgmental. Most of her relationships with men were short-lived; most of them were never quite able to live up to her high standards. At 35, she was going out with a nice, if rather boring, young CPA in Manhattan. He was somewhat intimidated by her, as were many of the men she had gone out with in the past.

Having worked her way up to the position of senior economist with a midsize New York commercial bank, Madeline had achieved significant success in her career. She knew how to be politically aggressive, yet deferential when necessary. She had made her career ambitions well known to those who could help her achieve them. Madeline had a net worth of more than a half million dollars, and she invested in the stocks of takeover candidates.

Her strategy for investing was straightforward. Madeline would pick five or six takeover candidates and assume sizable positions in each, knowing that three or four of them would never go anywhere. She reasoned that one or two would be big winners. As soon as the prospective winners' stocks started to rise, she'd automatically assume the others to be losers. But she never got rid of her position in the losers since they rarely lost very much and there was always the possibility that they could turn out to be winners.

When her one or two prized stocks rose, Madeline became excited and anxious, wondering when to sell. It was a question that plagued her. Many times, Madeline would sell out her winners before they reaped sizable profits. And those profits would be eroded by the losers she steadfastly held on to.

Though Madeline's net worth continued to grow, it was through her salary, not through her trading efforts.

Madeline's problem: She was afraid to win. This was her problem although she also hated to lose. Madeline had been afraid to be her class valedictorian, afraid to make a good impression in her interviews with Radcliffe and Yale, afraid to form a lasting relationship with a man.

She was also afraid to win too big at investing. Though she never lost big, she never won big either.

Madeline was a victim of the "toxicity" of success. To conflicted investors, success is toxic and anxiety is the symptom after they taste success. This anxiety when faced with success has been a pattern throughout Madeline's life.

What can she do about it? Madeline needs to become more comfortable with winning. Perhaps her strategy should be to win small amounts at first and then slowly and steadily increase the amount of her wins. As part of this strategy, she should make the decision to jettison her positions in companies she instinctively knows will be losers.

Conflicted investors can't handle success. Many people say, "If I won the lottery, I certainly wouldn't have any trouble spending the money." Yet all the studies on people who suddenly acquire wealth demonstrate that it's a very stressful situation. If you're conflicted, the situation becomes toxic.

Unlike some of the other psychological obstacles that negatively affect investors, conflict isn't a "loud" one. We've found that conflicted investors such as Madeline tend to internalize rather than externalize their emotions. Conflict is a vague and puzzling malady, and as a result, investors don't bemoan their losses and wring their hands in public. They tend to suffer silently. If you see yourself in this portrait—if Madeline's story is your own—don't despair. Conflicts can be resolved. One of the keys to its resolution is recognizing the anxiety that's catalyzed by success.

THE OEDIPAL CYCLE

You make a trade or take a position and it's successful. You're pleased. The next trade is also successful, and you're even more pleased. In fact, you're excited.

At this point, you might become a bit anxious that something "bad" will happen. Subsequently, you make a small mistake and suffer a loss. It's a loss that brings with it an inaudible sigh of relief. Still, you dig in your heels and vow not to make the mistake again.

But of course, you do. The cycle repeats itself. Win, lose, win, lose. It's the Oedipal game. When you win, you smell blood. Win some more and you sense the possibility of taking over, of being in charge as Oedipus was in charge after he killed his father and married his mother. That's why you become anxious. And that's why you make a mistake—you don't have to deal with the tremendous anxiety produced by constant winning.

Again, most of this is unconscious. But most of you can recognize the investment pattern. Think about how your lucky streak ended, how you felt. It probably wasn't bad luck that ended your streak. More likely, you ended it yourself.

OBJECTS OF ENVY

Conflict can manifest itself in many ways. One of the most common conditions, and one that affects many investors, is an inferiority complex. This isn't always easily acknowledged; many people disguise their inner feeling of inferiority with "outer" superiority. Nonetheless, they harbor serious doubts about their abilities. These doubts lead to envy, and the investment environment behaves like a magnet in drawing envy out of you. Envy is fine if you recognize it for what it is. If you don't, it can overwhelm you, pulling you toward bad investment decisions and away from sound ones.

What investor doesn't believe that there are great, successful traders/investors out there? They have the secret, the power, the information, allowing them to secure what is rightly ours. It's not the money we envy as much as the investment wizard's mysterious skill at making it. It's that fantasized skill that the envious investor feels the desire to possess.

When our money manager wins, we are elated that we've connected ourselves with the right expert. When he or she loses, we resentfully blame the loss on ourselves. We say, "I should have seen that [s]he didn't have what it takes! [S]He didn't use open interest, timing cycles, Gann angles, or Elliot Wave theory. I should've picked someone who did."

FEELING LIKE DAMAGED GOODS

You feel deficient. Envy does that to you. Unconsciously, you're thinking: "What have I done that makes me a loser in this way? Am I being punished for something I did wrong? Was I too greedy?"

So you assume you need help. You need a good broker, a magical trader, a better system. Something to make up for what you're missing.

It all boils down to bad investment judgment. Envious investors become timid. They hang back and wait for direction. They hesitate before buying or selling, and as any investor knows, "He who hesitates is lost." In response to the losses caused by hesitation, envious investors occasionally switch gears, becoming victims of impulsive, poorly planned gambles.

When, for example, the moving average strategy of switching no-load mutual funds advocated by a certain newsletter fails, you quickly give your remaining money to the next "hot" money manager who comes along. You're thinking, "Somebody (other than me) must have the right formula."

Other envious investors can't get off the dime. They are paralyzed. Even though they see good investment opportunities, they can't capitalize on them. Why? Because they don't trust their judgment. They're sure they'll be wrong, that they've overlooked something.

Envious investors become locked into a vicious cycle. To find what they're missing, they search for some investor guru who has it all. But even when they find such a person and they make a successful investment, they deem it a fluke. That's confirmed with the inevitable bad investment the guru eventually makes. A new guru is searched for, found, and the process repeats itself.

Ultimately, resignation sets in. Such investors feel they'll never win, no matter what they do. They are trapped by their envy.

ACTION PLAN FOR THE CONFLICTED INVESTOR

How do you escape this trap as well as all the others that are set by conflict? What do you do to return to your senses, to become a sensible investor?

Begin by identifying your conflict. It's not as difficult as you might think. Consider your internal debates, your emotions, and your characteristic ways of handling painful events. Such consideration will yield the ingredients of your conflict.

As we discussed in Chapter 4, "The Mind/Money Journal," most of you keep charts or records of your investments and trades. Do the same thing with your personal observations related to investing. Chart your emotional reactions and thoughts alongside your trades. Identify your feelings about each trade, before and after you make it. See if you can extract the crucial theme of your investing and trading life as you log in your wishes, criticisms, emotions, and defenses. Pay particular attention to the "anxiety" or agitation that you feel. It's a critical clue that your conflict is brewing and may well be affecting your trading.

Case Study

Marty S., Conflicted Investor

Marty S., 32 years old and married, is wealthy, having inherited $40 million. He feels that he has a good heart and a good business head. He has altruistically helped turn around a struggling home for battered women, using his business and marketing acumen as well as his money. However, Marty wishes he could do more.

Marty has also invested in several business partnerships but has enjoyed little success. He mostly breaks even, and sometimes loses money. Recently, Marty entered into a business partnership with Steve, a 39-year-old entrepreneur who had ambitious plans to establish cable television programming from midnight to 1:00 A.M. "One Hour of Midnight Delight" was the theme of the project. Steve convinced Marty that he could use the profits from this venture to fund additional shelters for the homeless. Marty decided to invest $400,000 into the project.

Steve quickly hired several employees, leased expensive cars, and rented prime commercial real estate for his offices. After six months, the multiple contracts that Steve had expected did not pan out. He asked Marty for an additional $50,000 investment.

Before sinking more money into the project, Marty decided to review his mind/money journal. His entries were revealing. A sample follows:

Recent Events

I took the kids to the new zoo today, and they loved it. I'd like to do something to help out there. Steve *called and asked for another $50,000—I told him about the zoo idea, and he didn't seem interested. He seems to be totally preoccupied with "Midnight Delight."*

I received a business proposal from a group of physicians who want to start a "preventive health watch" network. The network would operate an 800-number service to provide information on health issues such as cholesterol, blood sugar, high blood pressure, etc. To do so, they would need $350,000. They have also agreed not to receive any payment or profit monies until I have been paid back in full. After that, I would receive 30% of the profits, while they kept 70%.

Thoughts

I like the zoo.
I'm upset with Steve.
I'm tired of getting bamboozled, but how do I know these doctors won't use me as well?
I've got to cut Steve off.

Emotions

Anxious (guilty?) around Steve.
Hopeful about the zoo.
Cautious about the health network project and the doctors.
Angry at Steve.

After looking at his journal entries, Marty concluded that he would "cut bait" with Steve and talk to the doctors about a "phased in" investment with them because he had recently been burned. By consulting his journal, he realized that he had been lumping his physicians' well-thought out and well-managed plan in with his experience with

Steve. He decided to take a "middle-road" approach with the new investors and cut his other losses. He also decided to become a member of the new zoo's board of directors. Marty is a conflicted investor: He feels guilty about his inherited wealth and yet has ambitious goals. However, he often winds up in a "zero-sum game"—doing "good" (achieving his goals) and yet losing money in the process. His mind/money journal has enabled him to identify his psychological mistakes more quickly and move progressively toward winning investments.

DREAMS AS GUIDES TO MANAGING CONFLICT

Another step involves paying attention to your dreams. Freud said that dreams were the "royal road" to the unconscious. You don't have to walk in the shoes of a psychiatrist to travel that road. Anyone can discern the plot of even the most bizarre dream and identify feelings about the dream.

Together, that plot and your feelings constitute a theme. Are there recurrent themes in your dreams? If so, that's a key to unlocking your conflict.

Pay particular attention to dreams that occur during tough investment decisions. Don't expect the dream to duplicate an investment scenario; it's unlikely that while you're contemplating a major stock purchase, you'll have a dream about a fire fueled by the stock certificates you were contemplating. Ah, you think, bad investment: If I make it, my money will go up in smoke. If only dreams were such clear communicators!

They communicate in a different way. But once you become comfortable with the language, you can understand the investment implications. For example, you're offered a real estate opportunity, and it sounds terrific. Your cousin, who also happens to be your accountant, can get you two condos at a 20 percent discount from an over-extended developed in New England. Even with a $200 negative monthly cash flow, you'll break even because of the tax write-off. All you have to do is hold on until the market improves. But you're worried about rising interest rates, about a declining real estate market. You struggle all day with the decision and decide to sleep on it.

That night, you dream of a large building with many floors. You're trying to get downstairs to a party, but you're blocked by construction in the stairwell. You backtrack, take another route, then run into your secretary. You realize that your attempt to get downstairs is dangerous and you're glad to see your secretary's familiar face.

You have a second dream. You're walking on a pier and board a large, old houseboat with many storefronts. They're all closed, so you walk to the front of the boat. You climb a scaffold. Suddenly, you realize how high you are and become scared. A young man appears and throws you a rope. You slide down and go into a cabin, where you meet the man's mother. They both seem familiar.

Both these dreams are about trying to get somewhere. Both times you encounter dangerous construction. Both times you find helpful people who show you a less dangerous route. Your fears are relieved.

You extract the plot and emotions from your dreams. You think: My fears and impulsive nature have caused me trouble with option trading in the past. Maybe that's why I'm hesitant about the real estate deal.

You pay attention to the dream theme: "Seemingly dangerous journeys can be made less fearful by helpful allies." You realize that your worries about the deal—rising interest rates, a declining real estate market—are more than offset by the faith you have in your cousin. Based on past experience, you accept that your cousin is shrewd, experienced, and successful when it comes to real estate. So you decide to buy the condos, and they turn out to be a great investment.

The third step in this process involves paying attention to your feelings during the three phases of an investment. When you consider your alternatives prior to the investment, are you excited, apprehensive, frightened? As you actually make the investment—as you buy or sell—how do you feel? When the deal is done, how do you feel afterward—happy with the gain, sad at the loss, indifferent? Your feelings, together with your dream theme, will clue you into what's really affecting your investing.

CONSULT WITH HELPFUL OTHERS . . . INCLUDING YOUR PRIVATE SELF

Question your underlying motives. What are your wishes regarding an investment? Does the investment seem to be of enormous importance; of significance far beyond what it really should be? Watch out! Are you indifferent to the investment? Watch out! Smooth investment sailing means navigating between the rock of the wish and the hard place of the internal critic.

Second, are there people you're not discussing the investment with? Your spouse, family, best friend? Why? Is there some discomfort involved in sharing your thoughts? That's a telltale sign that something is wrong.

Third, discover your role model. Our survey revealed that *successful investors with conflicted personalities have investing role models.* Though a role model doesn't guarantee success, it is clearly a great advantage for those of you who are conflicted. Perhaps it's an advantage because such a model provides you with a beacon through the fog of conflict; you can rely on the advice of an observer with investing skills who is outside the conflict that otherwise would obscure your investing decisions. If you don't have an investor role model, search for one. Don't randomly grab the hottest market guru out there, the one that's all sizzle and no steak. Instead, look for someone whose style matches your style, who shares your values. Don't worry if your model isn't the world's most well-known investor. In fact, the model can and perhaps should be someone with whom you can develop a real, personal relationship. Choose the person whose advice and outlook on investing make sense to you. Analyze this individual's investing philosophy, strategy, and tactics. Are they logical? Have they worked well for this person and others who have followed his or her recommendations?

Fourth, you might want to consider psychotherapy and psychoanalysis; these disciplines are extremely helpful at resolving conflicts in all types of people. They are not a quick fix, but they can have an extraordinarily positive long-term effect on your attitude toward and investment of your money. If you choose not to work with a professional, then it's advisable to find some other confidant. Based on our experience, conflicted investors can benefit greatly if they "open up" to someone else—a friend, a spouse, a role model. Bringing the conflict into the light, rather than letting it do harm in the dark, is a first step to overcoming the negative effects it can have on your investing/trading decisions.

CHAPTER 10

The Depressed Investor

Happy investors tend to be successful investors. The Garfield–Epstein survey revealed that most people who do well in the financial markets are relatively happy people. That doesn't mean they don't get depressed occasionally or that they don't have their bad days. Generally, however, the people who win have blue sky rather than grey sky outlooks.

There's a psychological and investing logic behind this finding. If you're investing under a cloud of depression, your perception of risks and rewards becomes warped; the risks seem bigger, the rewards seem smaller. If you make investment decisions guided by this dark perception, you will probably make equally dark decisions.

Similarly, depression breeds apathy and resignation. Your broker tells you about a hot new stock and you shrug your shoulders, saying, "Yeah, well, I don't think any new company is going to do well in this economy." Or you find that your strategy isn't paying off as well as it did in the past, and you resign yourself to its decreasing ineffectiveness rather than adjust your strategy.

Your investing judgment is affected. Potential winners and losers all look the same to the depressed investor. You're like someone whose taste buds have been dulled—you can't tell the difference between garlic and onion. When you can't differentiate between IBM and ABC Computer, you're in trouble.

SIGNS OF DEPRESSION

Do you exhibit at least five of the classic signs of depression? Look over the following list and see how many apply to you:

- Depressed mood: down, blue, in a funk.
- Loss of pleasure.
- Disturbed appetite: significant, unintentional weight loss or gain.
- Poor libido: no sex drive.
- Loss of usual interests: a lifelong passion for football watching disappears, for instance.
- Low energy.
- Social withdrawal.
- Suicidal thoughts.
- Hopelessness.
- Sleep disturbance: waking up very early.

Now examine another type of list. This one relates to typical feelings of depression during the investing process. Check the attitudes that apply to you:

- Feeling detached from your trading system (you don't have any positive or negative emotions about it; it's just there, a tool).

- Not pursuing specific reasons for your losses (you just accept them without investigating or thinking about what went wrong).

- Failing to follow up on new investing/trading ideas.

- Feeling chronically burned out during the investing process.

- Being "late" (missing turns in the market that you would usually be on top of, e.g., selling too late, being too late to enter a trade).

- Following your trading system by rote without thinking about how it might be improved (this is different from breaking discipline; here, you simply refuse to question a system that should be questioned).

- Not doing your usual information-gathering (failing to read newsletters or to lunch with people who might give you trading tips and advice).

- Eating a lot less—or more—than usual during trading.

- Worrying excessively about losses.

- Staying awake nights or getting up early, disturbed by investing or trading matters.

- Taking no pleasure in winning.

- Feeling down when market goes up.

- Feeling constant guilt about not winning enough, not being a good enough investor.

If five or more of the preceding items apply to you, and five or more of the symptoms on the psychological list also apply, you're probably a depressed investor. The next step is figuring out the type of depression that is causing you to perform below your investing potential. The three types of depression—biological, psychological, and social—all have different causes and "cures." Let's examine each one.

Case Study

Susan R., A Biologically Depressed Investor

Susan R. moved rapidly upward in the banking world. At Smith as an undergraduate and the Wharton School as a graduate student, Susan received top grades. She came from an upper middle-class family, growing up on Philadelphia's affluent Main Line. Her mother was a hospital personnel director, and her father was a lawyer. Her mother had a scare from breast cancer, but has been free of symptoms for the past five years. Her father was a diagnosed manic-depressive, but his condition has stabilized by taking Lithium.

After receiving her MBA, Susan had a number of attractive job offers, finally settling on a career in finance. Unhappy and bored as a credit analyst with a Japanese bank based in Philadelphia, she moved into their investment banking division and quickly decided she wanted to be a portfolio manager. Susan was astute in sizing up companies and had a good eye for charting business cycles of various industries.

By the time Susan was 29, she was rapidly approaching the upper echelons of bank management. After two years as assistant to the over-the-counter portfolio manager, she'd been appointed head of the entire investment division. At first, she did a great job—up 20 percent by Labor Day. She'd been well-positioned in steels, machinery, and agriculturals. Susan was considered a rising star, and it was said that she had the "touch"— everything she bought into turned to gold.

Her personal life, too, was going well. She'd been dating a real estate lawyer named Mark, and marriage and kids were in their future.

Looking back, it would have been impossible to predict what would happen to Susan. The only trouble spot in her life had been a period in college when she went a little wild—sleeping with a number of men, pulling all-nighters, going on spending sprees where she would charge piles of new clothes, a television, even a new car on her parents' credit cards. When her parents found out, they had a series of talks with her and she snapped out of it, becoming the Susan they had always known. Her parents decided that Susan had just been going through a rebellious phase. As a relatively introverted math major with a business career in mind, Susan returned to her typical self.

At the age of 30, however, Susan began behaving atypically. After the stress of the third-quarter reports was over, she found herself unable to come down from the hectic, previous weeks. She was wound up, waking early, losing weight rapidly. More troublesome from a work perspective, she felt "out of gas." She couldn't concentrate on all those reports of initial public offerings. She left piles of 10K's on her desk, not even bothering to give them a cursory glance.

Susan begged off dates with Mark and spent weekends at home, not doing much of anything. She worried about her health—could that persistent cough be the sign of something more serious? At work, Susan was indecisive. As she tried to determine the industries that would benefit from expansion—focusing on the entertainment and telecommunications groups—she found herself strangely unsure. For every argument in favor of those groups, she marshaled an argument against them—casino profit margins were increasing, but on the other hand, some pending laws might cut into those margins. Back and forth she went, unable to control the pendulum. When the industry groups under consideration finally went down, Susan not only sold too late, but she had nothing else on the board and felt desperate.

Susan's depression was biological. Her family history, her manic phase in college, and her present behavior, present clear signs. If unheeded, her emotional and investment prognosis is poor.

BIOLOGICAL DEPRESSION

To determine if you, like Susan, are suffering from biological depression that's playing havoc with your investing results, look for these additional signs and symptoms:

- A family history of depression or manic-depression.
- Severe mood changes within a daily time frame, characterized by feelings of almost debilitating lethargy and sudden returns to "normalcy."
- Trouble with concentration and memory.
- That out-of-gas feeling—feeling like a vegetable.
- Slow thoughts—no energy.

Case Study

Peter C., A Psychologically Depressed Investor

Peter had grown up in a wealthy northern Chicago suburb, the son of a corporate executive. Single and 41, Peter had never been married— except to his job. He traded bonds at the Chicago Board of Trade and also filled orders for a few large institutions.

Peter had been a trader all his adult life. He had started working at the CBOT as a runner during the summer before his senior year at college; he never finished his BA. Like many others, he worked his way up through the system, taking phone orders, working as a local, obtaining more brokering business on the floor, getting known, watching and learning. He was also good at saving his money.

Peter had seen slumps before—lasting weeks or even months—but nothing like now. He had gone through six months of losses with no end in sight. He added 30 pounds to his already hefty frame because of the anxiety. Luckily, during the bull market in bonds in the early and mid-1980s, Peter had saved a good deal of money. Still, his heavy losses were eroding his savings. Since it was a trading market, Peter had been using his spread program. But he continually got whipsawed and stopped out.

Eight months ago, Peter had been in intensive negotiations with one of his clients, a global investment broker; he had been handling their business in the bond pit for a number of years. The brokerage firm's head of U.S. operations had approached Peter about directing the company's U.S. commodities division. Steve, the director of U.S. operations, had met with Peter and explained what the company was looking for: a hard-working person, knowledgeable about commodities, who possessed common sense, and could see through systems and programs, while not losing sight of the bottom line. Peter seemed to fit the bill.

The job fell through. Steve's corporate bosses balked at putting someone in the position who lacked a college degree. Peter was disappointed. His involvement with his own trading waned.

Peter still followed his spread system, but when it failed, he did not attempt to analyze why: He just chalked it up to trading losses. Instead of trying to work out the bugs or trying to readjust his stops, Peter waited for the market to come around. He knew the importance of discipline and following one's system.

But Peter wasn't paying attention to his system—he was detached from it. He was depressed and didn't know it.

Peter's father had never finished college and wanted, more than anything else, for his children to be well-educated professionals: doctors, lawyers, professors. It seemed that nothing Peter did besides bringing home good grades could satisfy his father. Peter's creativity, determination, common sense, and other good qualities escaped his father's notice.

Peter loved and admired his father and, in a way, had followed in his father's footsteps: His dad had worked his way up the corporate ladder in the same fashion that Peter had risen through the ranks at the Board of Trade.

Through all his success as a trader, Peter never felt like a success—not in his father's eyes or his own. When the possibility of a professional job arose, Peter saw it as his last chance to grab the gold ring that might return his father's love. When the turn of the carousel took the ring beyond reach, Peter was devastated.

Even worse was the financial devastation Peter's trades were suffering. His good judgment was gone. In the past, when one of his systems stopped working, he would look for the sources of trouble, even as he stayed with it. He'd ask: Was it the market, the system, or my own flawed thinking that is causing the problem? Now he asked none of those questions. Though he felt bad about the losses, he couldn't take action.

Peter's problem can be diagnosed as psychological, as opposed to social or biological, because of the absence of biological or medical symptoms and the presence of a precipitating event (the loss of a job opportunity) and the history of a major conflict with a parent.

PSYCHOLOGICAL DEPRESSION

- No biological or medical symptoms.
- Clear-cut precipitating event such as the loss of job, spouse, opportunity.
- History of unresolved wishes with a parent.

Case Study
Candace M., A Socially Depressed Trader

Candace had just about everything: fancy house in Rye, New York, attentive husband, three adorable children, and the freedom to do what she wanted. Which she did. Candace traveled to Europe each year and enjoyed trading crude oil futures on the New York Mercantile Exchange. Her father had been vice-president of one of the largest U.S. oil companies and had left her and her family a sizable inheritance. Although her husband didn't need to work, he was a quite successful oil man himself. He owned controlling interest in a successful investment group that structured gas/oil partnerships for major U.S. and foreign brokerage houses. So, Candace had always lived in the oil world and knew a fair amount about the forces that moved the market. And she was fairly successful at predicting price movements.

Yet, things changed for Candace when the kids got older and she and her husband decided to move into downtown Manhattan. They figured that with the vast cultural opportunities that the city provided, both of them would be happier as the children became progressively more independent. Candace, who was excited about the move, threw herself into the tasks of furnishing and decorating the new apartment, and she even visited the exchange itself a few times to see the action firsthand. After a few weeks, Candace noted that she wasn't so interested in visiting the trading floor. Although she called her friends in Rye, it was more difficult to get together. Her husband was still busy at work and he had his life there to fall back on, but Candace felt that something was missing. Her trading suffered as well. She just didn't have the kind of enthusiasm and vitality for the oil markets that she used to possess. Even the kids noticed it. "Mom, you always look so bummed out. Don't you like the new house?" In fact, Candace loved the new condo, but it was her new life that depressed her—worse yet, she didn't even know she was depressed because she couldn't figure out what might be wrong.

And, she was now losing money in the markets. She wasn't able to enter trades as she had; her timing on entry was way off. She would buy not at the trough but well into the rise and get executed on her stops in the pull-backs. She was losing all the time. She wondered whether visiting the floor was having a bad influence on her

timing. She avidly looked for all sorts of explana-
tions. She realized that she was irritated with her
husband's delight at now being in the city, but she
didn't know why. Candace was suffering from a
"socially based" depression and didn't know it.

SOCIAL DEPRESSION

- Recent change in social circumstances: family changes, geographical moves, new job, financial windfall, or shortfall.
- Problem seems social rather than psychological: leading relatively well-adjusted life, no apparent psychological losses or repeating of old, bad patterns.

You may have a change in social scene that you think should make you happy but it turns out that it makes you sad. Or you may be ignoring the impact of your social environment altogether. A social depression shows no repetition or repeating psychological pattern. You simply need to get yourself out of what you've gotten yourself into! You need to make changes—now!

ACTION PLAN FOR THE DEPRESSED INVESTOR

Rule out Biological Depression

- *See Your Doctor.* Make sure that you don't have thyroid or other endocrine problems or that you are not taking medications with side effects of sluggishness or depression.
- *Consider Seeing a Psychiatrist.* See if you have a biological depression that will respond to antidepressant medication or lithium.

Consider Psychological Depression

- *Check Your Mind/Money Journal.* See if a specific trading or investing event or other interpersonal event has triggered your lack of enthusiasm for the markets.
- *Check with Spouses or Friends.* See if they think something might be going on with you that could cause you to be down and pessimistic about your trading.
- *Study Your Personal Money Timeline.* Spot recurrent patterns or contributing factors from your past that have triggered your funk.
- *Get Counseling/Psychotherapy.* A consultation may help to sort through things quickly.

Change Your Environment—Shake It Up!

- *Check your Mind/Money Journal.* Identify recent social changes.
- *Make Changes in People.* Get divorced, get married, get new friends, get rid of old ones, fire people, hire people, transfer to a new boss, or get a new broker.
- *Make Changes in Spaces.* These could include bedroom, office, home, brokerage house, or car.
- *Make Changes in Work/Activities.* Quit your job, get a new job, add on new activities, cut back on the number of things you're trying to do, join new organizations, quit old ones, or start new hobbies.

INVESTING AND TRADING STRATEGIES FOR THE DEPRESSED INVESTOR

1. *Stop Trading.* Wait until you are undepressed. You don't need to be a Pollyanna to resume your financial involvements, but until you are well on your way out of your depressed state, your net worth will decline at the same rate as your self-worth. At the very least, cut

back on the amounts you are investing until you feel
your spirits lifting.

2. *Check Your Trades or Investments with People You
Trust.* Let them take control of your market activity
(with your approval) so that the slower pace you have
adopted doesn't work against you. Of course, never
hand over all your money to someone you don't know
or trust completely.

3. *Check Your Journal.* Identify any daily mood patterns. Perhaps you feel up in the morning but begin to
slide in the afternoon, or vice versa. If so, then try to
complete your trading before lunch. Try not to invest
when your mood is low.

4. *Use an Automatic System for Awhile.* It will put you in
at preset entry points and get you out at preset exit
points. Using a system will enable you to avoid the
devastating indecisiveness of your depression.

5. *Muster up Your Anger and Get Mad at the Markets!* In
psychoanalysis, when a patient displays depression, the
therapist looks for the anger behind it. When you are
depressed and losing, get angry about the financial
beating you are taking. If yours is a psychological depression (like Peter's), getting mad at those who have
disappointed you can be helpful. Venting that anger can
sometimes clear the way toward the path of recovery—
and successful investing.

CHAPTER 11

The Revenging Investor

Almost everyone who has ever invested has had losses. You have probably heard the pros tell that you should suffer these mishaps gracefully.

We think it is impossible to follow that "advice."

Who can accept a dramatic and costly stock drop with grace and equanimity? Only the sainted few, and we assume you're not among them. It's normal to react to loss with sadness or anger. Nobody likes to lose.

Revenging investors, however, are unable to shake the pain of loss. Somewhere in the back of their minds is a scorecard. They think, "If I make $2000 on this quick option trade, then I'll be even for the year." Instead of using a successful formula to determine where they'll invest, revenging investor's allow their need to "get even" make the trade instead.

There is an old Wall Street adage: "Never marry a stock." But all too frequently, investors end up treating 200 shares of IBM like a spouse or a lover. When the price goes up, the investor loves the beauty of the shares even more. But when the price goes down, the same investor feels seduced, abandoned, and most devastating of all, betrayed.

How do you handle betrayal? How do you prevent it from turning you into someone who invests with all the objectivity of a cuckold?

REVENGE HAS A LONG SHELF LIFE

A friend of ours was in love with a beautiful, strong-willed woman. He courted her, charmed her, and finally, almost won her over. At first, she thought he was a nice guy. Very cute and funny. But she was looking for someone more intense. They dated, they got closer, and just when it seemed as if they might really become seriously involved with each other, she pulled away.

His response was to be cool on the outside and adopt a socially acceptable attitude: "It just wasn't meant to be. She's got a lot of things to work out. I'm not sure she was really right for me," and so on. Inside, however, it was a different story. He was furious, unable to escape the pain and loss.

Five years later, after he had become seriously involved with someone else, he was asked about his old paramour. Initially, he didn't respond. Then he was asked, "Have you forgiven her? Do you remember what happened?" He answered, "I *don't* forgive and I *can't* forget."

Revenge lurks in the corners of the mind waiting for an apology: a deep, honest, actual apology. Revenge is born in the people who view their loss as a heartless betrayal. Such people often feel that to recover or move on, they must receive something, like an apology, from whoever or whatever spurned them. The investors who experience loss as a betrayal are asking for trouble. That's because the market is a spiteful lover. It does *not* apologize. You might care for it, but there's no guarantee that it will care for you in return. If you invest to seek revenge and wait for your apology, you'll have a long wait.

THE REVENGING PROFILE

Our survey revealed two important pieces of information about revenging investors: (1) They are likely to be very unsuccessful investors; (2) the way to success for this type of investor is paved by a mentor.

Based on our survey, revenging investors do not have much success with investments. Perhaps that's because so much of their energy is diverted by their out-to-get-even, got-to-beat-the-market, gonna-finally-get-wealthy mentality. Revenge is all consuming. More so than most other mind-over-money types, the revenging investor is dominated by this quest to triumph over an adversary. You don't have to look further than Shakespeare's tragic protagonists to see how revenge turns otherwise intelligent, perceptive people into tunnel-visioned, bloodthirsty creatures. The revenging investor lacks good judgment when it comes to investing (as well as many other matters).

Yes, revenge is a source of energy. But it's often misdirected energy. "Vengeance is mine," sayeth the Lord, "I shall repay." Unfortunately, vengeance doesn't pay. If you'll recall, the knights who went on holy crusades didn't fare too well.

FIND A MENTOR

You can turn the negative aspects of your revenging type into a positive. Like the conflicted investor, your solution is to find a mentor. Almost uniformly, our revenging respondents who had a mentor were successful investors.

From a psychological standpoint, this makes sense for a number of reasons. First, it gives you someone who can help you harness all the energy produced by a vengeful mind-set. Instead of focusing all that combustible anger at getting even, a mentor can assist you in concentrating on getting ahead.

Second, there's nothing like some sage advice from someone you respect to put your revenge and its precipitating cause in perspective. Think of a time when you were disappointed in love—your girlfriend or boyfriend broke off the relationship. You talked to a friend, or an older brother, or a sister who said, "Yeah, I can remember when I got dumped. I thought I would never recover. All I wanted to do was to make him pay dearly. But I got over it. You'll find someone else, and in a while, you'll have trouble understanding why you were so angry at what [s]he did."

Your trading mentor will echo that sentiment: "Don't dwell on how the market beat you today. Get a fresh start tomorrow. If you try and trade based on what happened in the past, you're not going to have much of a future. you can't do anything about that stock's unexpected plunge, so don't try. There are other stocks out there that you'll fall in love with, and if you choose wisely, they'll love you back."

Case Study

Dr. B.—A Revenging Investor

Dr. B. is an orthopedic surgeon. He figured that if he could go through medical school and residency at the top of his class, option trading should be a cinch.

He followed two or three high-tech stocks and when he thought one was in a bull move, he bought calls. He had a system: If he lost 50 percent of the option value, he would sell out. But he rarely did. He would average down. And five

times out of six, he would lose his entire investment or sell out after an 80 percent loss of all
capital.

Why? Was he stupid or simply undisciplined?
Neither. He was investing out of revenge. Theo-
retically, he understood what he needed to do.
But emotionally, he couldn't implement his system. He wanted to get even. His beloved high-
tech stock option had disappointed him and he
could not bear it. The union had to be right. Everything had been arranged.

You're probably wondering why Dr. B.
couldn't take the losses. The fact is that he *could*
take the losses—he *did* take the losses. It was the
betrayal that he couldn't take.

USING THE PERSONAL MONEY TIMELINE TO IDENTIFY REVENGE

The problem with identifying mind-over-money factors
such as revenge is that the roots are often buried in your
past. They're sunk so far back in time that if you merely
look at your life now you can't see them. When you draw
your money timeline, however, you get to glimpse factors
such as revenge and see how they grew and took hold of
your investing.

Let's briefly review the structure of a money timeline. Start by drawing a horizontal line on a blank page of
your mind/money journal. Divide it into segments
marked in five-year blocks. Underneath each block, jot
down particular events, attitudes, and people related to
money in your life. Table 11–1 should remind you of how
to construct your timeline.

Table 11-1   Sarah's Personal Money Timeline

0	5	10
Dad working as car mechanic	Dad promoted to chief mechanic	
Mom at home with kids	Parents bought small house	
Money very tight	All money to mortgage	
Renting apartment	Mom worried about overstretch	
No savings	Mom guilty about house	
Family happy	Dad unconcerned	

10	15	20
Dad in same position	Sarah off to state college	
Mom starts work as secretary	Parents get separated	
Dad upset with mom's absence	Dad buys his own garage	
Parental fights about mom's job	Mom at same job	
Mom insists they need the money		

20	25	30
Sarah's parents divorced	Meet Alex and get married "on rebound"	
Dad buys second garage	Alex's family—"comfortable"	
Mom at same job	Buy small house	
Parents pay for her expenses	Alex finishes CPA	
Sarah dating John (wealthy)	Sarah learns programming	
Break up with John	Nancy is born (daughter)	

30	35	40
Sarah at home with Nancy	Thomas is born (son)	
Alex doing well as CPA	Spending a lot on child care	
Saving $5000 per year	Sarah part-time work	
Alex buys expensive boat	Alex promoted to partner	
Add on to house	Saving $5000 per year	

40	45	
Sarah promoted at work	Sarah starts trading stocks	
Live-in help	Sarah cuts back at work	
Alex has to travel as partner	Sarah helps Thomas with schoolwork	
Thomas has learning problem		

Case Study

Sarah H., Loyal to a Fault

Sarah, a married 45-year-old computer pro-
grammer, invests in high-tech stocks and does her
own research and trading. She feels knowledgeable about the companies she invests in, but she
has lost about $5000 over the past year due to
bad "timing"—she holds on to her losers too long.
Though she bought stocks in the past, this is the
first time she's traded stocks. Her husband teases
her about her trading but doesn't interfere. Sarah
has a 15-year-old daughter and an 11-year-old
son. She started trading as a way of making extra
money for her daughter to go to a private college.
She spends up to eight hours a day researching
the market but can't seem to stem her losses; she's
very frustrated about losing.

Looking at her timeline, Sarah notices that
she's been "burned" twice: Her happy childhood
was taken away by her mother's going to work as
a secretary and by her mother's unwarranted concern about money. Next, she was spurned by John
(and marries Alex on the rebound).

Inside, Sarah wants to get even—to get her
parents "undivorced" and to avoid having been
dumped. Unconsciously, she vows that daughter
Nancy won't have to go through the same emotional suffering; Sarah won't be away from home
because of work and won't betray her loyalties.

As Sarah reviews her timeline, she gains these
and other insights. She sees a pattern of loyalty in
her life—an almost doglike loyalty to people she
believes in and cares about. Could this loyalty extend to her investing, she wonders? Am I being

too loyal to my stocks, refusing to get rid of them even when I know I should?

The answer, of course, is yes. With this insight, Sarah's trading becomes more successful. No longer does she hold on to stocks that she knows in her heart and mind are losers. She must remind herself, "Stocks are not people—I can let them go." Before, when she thought about selling them, she'd be stopped cold by some unnameable feeling that she was making a mistake. Now, she can name the cause of that feeling: fear of being disloyal. This doesn't mean Sarah will quickly sell every stock at the drop of a hat. But she won't be trading based on decades-old feelings of revenge and betrayal.

SIGNS OF THE REVENGING PROFILE

When you construct your timeline, look for patterns. Scan the timeline for repeated feelings, attitudes, and actions. Look for the telltale signs of revenge. Those signs include:

- *Intense Anger at Others Because of Financial Slights.* You couldn't go to a private college or camp because your parents refused to help you financially; your boss didn't give you the raise you felt you deserved; you can't afford the luxury car you want because of family financial obligations.

- *A Desire to Get Even.* You engage in an intense debate with a superior who doesn't grant you a raise or bonus, vowing that he or she will regret it; a screaming match develops with your spouse when [s]he spends money on something that you had reserved for your own personal use.

- *The Desire to Make a Financial Killing.* It's not enough to win; you have to win big. You're willing to take big risks for big gains, often foolishly (with hindsight). You disdain small gains for a chance at the pot of gold.

- *Intense Loyalty.* You stick with your investments through thick and thin (mostly thin). You find yourself unable to sell a piece of property even though its value is obviously on the decline; you rationalize holding on to a stock even after your broker strongly advises you to sell.

If these signs recur in your timeline, consider the possibility that you're a revenging investor and that this desire for revenge is tainting your investing strategy.

REVENGE IN ROMANCE

One of the simplest methods to determine if you fit in the revenging category is to examine your romantic relationships. How would you answer the following questions:

- Have you ever been dumped?
- How did you handle rejection, especially if you invested a significant amount of time and emotion in the relationship?
- Did you become withdrawn or angry?
- How long did your mourning period last; was it more than a few weeks?
- Looking back on the rejection, does it still gall you, even though months or even years have passed?
- Do you fantasize about "getting even" with the person who dumped you, showing that person that he or she made a big mistake?
- Do you find yourself being unable to forgive and forget?

If you answered yes to most or all of these questions, your vengeful feelings might not be limited to relationships. They probably extend to your relationship with money. Think about how you approach your investments. Does the fear of betrayal—of a prized stock going south on you—hover in the back of your mind? Do you hold it too long and too tightly, as if the sheer force of your love for it will prevent it from performing poorly?

Now, take a look at another diagnostic tool that may confirm you suspicions that revenge is hampering your trading.

DREAMS OF REVENGE

Like the conflicted investor, a revenging investor can also look to dreams for important clues. Again, your dreams can be one of your most important investment indicators. You should focus not so much on the specifics but on the overall theme or emotions. Do you dream about a quest? A duel? A love triangle? Does your dream deal with defeat? Is the feeling one of satisfaction? Or is it indignation or rage?

These bits and pieces are more valuable than you might think. As Carl Jung once said, "A dream unanalyzed is like a letter unopened." As we've discussed, your dreams hold a bounty of inside information that you cannot afford to ignore.

Let's put dream analysis to work. Suppose you are an active investor in common stocks. You use a discount brokerage, do your own research, and trade 200 lots. You go both long or short and follow five stocks, but principally trade three of them. One is a biotechnology company, where you've bought 200 shares. It is quite volatile in terms of its stock price. You have heard that the company may make an announcement about a new cancer-fighting drug in the near future.

You have been burned by this stock as it fell from $45 to $15. The overall stock market has been in a topping process but is holding up. Three weeks ago the stock was at $19. It then rose to $22.50 while the overall market broke 8 percent. The stock has since dipped to 19¾ and now sits at $20. You've been following the stock for a year and it has based at $15 to $17 and appears to have broken out to the upside. You are now sitting with your 200 shares and are concerned that this may have been a false breakout. You have the following two dreams:

You are in California, sort of hovering over San Francisco, which is recovering from an earthquake. Your favorite spot is the Golden Gate Bridge. You want to land on the bridge. But a friendly guard tells you to wait, warning you that it's too busy and everyone is preoccupied with rebuilding. You wait awhile, then become impatient and land on the bridge anyway. You end up getting stuck in traffic and you can't get off. You feel the bridge sway. You panic and become upset with yourself for landing.

In your second dream, you are watching two dogs sniff at a piece of meat. It looks as if they are going to fight. Suddenly, one of them turns around and walks away. The second dog eats the meat. He then appears to be choking to death. You are aghast.

In drawing out the themes and emotions of the two dreams, we can see that both are about presumably desirable objects and the suffering that results after obtaining those objects. In both dreams, signs of caution were ignored. In the first dream, the warning was the earthquake. In the second dream, the competitor leaves the meat. It's also worth noting that both dreams evoked fear and panic.

As an investor, you can learn a great deal about the psychological motivations behind your decisions from dreams.

If you were to pay attention to the two dreams as they relate to the scenario we discussed earlier, you could conclude that the stock market's recent plunge is warning you to be cautious; that your emotional attachment to the biotech company is too high because what you really want is for it to make up for burning you earlier. Using the indicators from your dreams, you decide to sell at a breakeven price including commissions. You watch from the sidelines as the overall market continues to flounder and the rumor of the new drug produces no new advance in the stock price. In this happily-ever-after ending, you have used dream interpretation to help you trade a dangerous desire for revenge for real investment success.

If you had kept an investment journal, you might have gleaned similar information that would have helped you decide what to do about the biotech company's stock. Putting even the briefest thoughts or feelings to paper every day can reveal quite a bit.

With regard to our biotech stock example, your journal could have recorded your constant anxiety about holding the stock after its correction. It might have also noted your continued focus on the deteriorating economy and the fact that your overall expectations for the advance in the stock were fairly low.

After realizing this, you should have seen that the risk was definitely not worth the reward. More importantly, your real motives become clear. You are able to understand that it wasn't so much a successful trade that you were after—you were trying to make up for a past loss.

ACTION PLAN FOR THE REVENGING INVESTOR

You've reviewed your past timeline, interpreted your dreams and read between the lines of your journal. You realize that you are in fact hampered by a need to get even. Now what? Well, like many other troublesome conditions, in this case recognizing your problem is the first step in overcoming it. Once you've done that, you need to design an effective plan that will help you manage your need for revenge. There are three principal methods you can use to keep revenge from interfering with successful investing:

1. You can use psychotherapy to cure or neutralize your need for revenge.
2. You can rely on an automatic investment system that factors out your input.
3. You can be vigilant, attuned to your below-the-surface emotions.

Clearly, the first method—some kind of **psychological consultation** that allows you to become conversant with the roots of your wish to get even—cannot hurt. In as few as three or four sessions, an astute clinician can help you discover the source of this obstacle. Such a discovery will then alert you to potential pitfalls.

An **automatic system,** the second method, buys and sells for you based on predetermined entry and exit conditions. When a system is set up this way, your input is factored out. You will want to be careful though, and make sure that a revenge bias is not encoded into the system. Otherwise, you'll find yourself in the midst of disaster.

You can rely on a demanding, though effective, plan based on **constant vigilance.** This is an age-old way to prevent you from being your own worst enemy. Traders or investors can use the tools of dream analysis and an investment journal to strike back at inner forces, such as revenge, that are potentially harmful. However, you must conduct research in two directions: toward the investment and toward your propensity for revenge, ever alert for the telltale signs (found in dreams and your journal) signaling your revenge impulse at work.

Remember to pace yourself, too, and take needed vacation time. Get away from the intensity of your revenge. You might seek relief by watching competitive sporting events—let someone else engage in winning/losing behavior, and live vicariously through them.

Finally, get a mentor. This isn't always easy for revenging investors. After all, you're vengeful for a reason, and that reason could be betrayal by your father or a father figure: Your dad constantly belittled you; a teacher told you you'd never make it past high school; a boss fired you.

Yet a mentor may be just what you need. As our survey points out, successful revenging investors possess mentors who can thwart the negative influences of the revenging mentality. When you irrationally hold on to an investment past the point of logic, they can point out the error to you. When you make the mistake of trying to get even with the market, they can explain the danger of your strategy.

A mentor, by definition, is someone you listen to and trust. Mere advisors can point out your errors but you may dismiss their advice, since their status isn't high enough to steer you away from your revenging course. But a mentor can break through the barriers your mind erects; he or she can put a check on your revenging tendencies.

Here's an example of how a mentor aided a revenging investor.

Case Study

Danny G., Determined to "Beat the Market"

Danny G. is a 27-year-old lawyer for a large Midwest legal firm. Single and handsome, Danny dates a lot, but his relationships don't last long. On more than one occasion, Danny had been dumped, which he hated; it reminded him of unpleasant childhood memories—when he was 11, his mother had left his dad for another man.

Danny started trading stock-index futures last year. In his first month, he made $55,000. He even contemplated leaving the law firm and trading full-time. But during the next 11 months, he lost all the money he made, though he did so through a series of exciting if ultimately unrewarding losses and gains. Danny was convinced he could become wealthy as a trader; it was just a matter of time before he beat the market.

Danny's father didn't approve of his trading, but Danny didn't pay much attention to his father's objections. After all, his dad had scoffed at Danny's earlier ambition to become an attorney. His father was a railroad worker, and he never believed that Danny could cut it financially and academically in law school.

The next year, during a particularly tumultuous swing in the markets, Danny stayed with a short position convinced that the market was topping. During a two-week period, the market pushed ahead 150 points, forcing Danny into a margin call and a $25,000 loss. He didn't have the money, and he couldn't borrow it.

Danny was despondent, and his mood affected his work at the firm. One of the senior partners, George L., noticed that Danny wasn't himself. He called Danny into his office and asked if everything was okay.

Uncharacteristically, Danny broke down crying at the question, spilling out the story of his trading loss. George's interest turned out to be more than a superior's concern for a subordinate's work performance. George was aware that Danny had been investing in futures; another associate had mentioned Danny's $55,000 windfall to him. For many years, George had dabbled in the markets and done pretty well for himself. He told Danny about his investing hobby, and he said he considered Danny a valuable member of the firm and would talk to the other partners about Danny's problem.

A few days later, George met Danny for lunch and said the firm would loan him $25,000 under two conditions. First, Danny must work an extra 20 hours a week for the next three months. Second, if Danny intended to continue trading, he must do so more conservatively.

To help Danny fulfill the second condition, George suggested that they meet after work and discuss Danny's trading strategy.

Over the next few weeks, George came up with a strategy that Danny adhered to: trading two contracts instead of one, keeping his stops tight and disciplined, and taking half-profits by selling one of the two contracts when he was ahead.

By following George's advice, Danny did reasonably well. None of his gains equaled the initial $55,000 bonanza, but at least he was ahead of the game. At first, Danny bridled under the strategy—the rush he felt when taking big risks wasn't there. Gradually, however, he adjusted to his new strategy and learned to get as much pleasure out of his small triumphs as he had over his one huge success.

DON'T GET EVEN—GET SMART

Danny learned his lesson the hard way: you can't get even with the market. At least, you can't get even in the sense that Danny wanted to get even. The market, or any given investing vehicle, is an inanimate object. Trying to "beat it" is like banging your head against the wall—the wall doesn't care. This type of investing strategy is doomed to failure because you are taking risks for the reward of vengeance, not for the reward of money.

You can't stop yourself from being a revenging investor; it's who you are. In fact, your trading/investing style offers certain advantages. You gain energy, competitiveness, a willingness to take risks. All these traits can stand you in good stead if they're channeled in the right direction. A mentor can help you channel them.

CHAPTER 12

The Masked Investor

Do you ever find yourself in a situation where you act differently than you normally do? Perhaps it's when you're with someone you're trying to impress, for example, your boss. Perhaps it's when you're with a group of people whose lifestyle is at odds with your own and you're trying to conform.

Whatever the situation, you realize with hindsight, "That's not me." Or perhaps someone who knows you well and has observed your behavior comments, "Why were you acting so strangely?" Consciously or unconsciously, you're "artificially" taking on a new persona. It's like pulling on a mask. You feel you need a disguise to deal effectively with a given environment.

From our survey, we found that there is a group of investors and traders who do the same thing. They alter who they are in the belief that an investing environment demands a new self: The shy, retiring type becomes an extraordinarily aggressive investor, or the risk-taking competitor becomes an overly cautious trader.

"Masked" investors, however, end up investing in competition with themselves. Our survey showed that masked investors often are confused, their confidence eroding as their disguises break down—as they invariably do.

To get a better sense of who this masked investor is, let us tell you Grace's story.

Case Study

Grace M., Many-Sided Trader

One of the few women who have been traders at the Chicago Mercantile Exchange, Grace M. was born in Hungary and came to Chicago at age 10 years. Her mother, a beautiful woman, had fled from the Nazis and after several years of living with distant relatives in New York, came to Chicago and remarried.

Though Grace was 50, she looked as if she was 35. She was regarded by other traders as loud and aggressive on the floor, but she was quiet and reclusive away from work. Her mother had emphasized the importance of being competitive, capable, and secure, and her belief about how a woman should conduct herself in the world was not lost on Grace. As a fairly successful T-bond trader, Grace had been discovered five years ago by a charismatic money manager and was now part of a five-person trading team managing over $5 million.

Grace prided herself on being thorough and precise. She researched credit markets carefully, including all foreign as well as domestic developments. Though she considered herself well-informed and level-headed, Richard, her boss, believed she was too cautious. He felt that her discipline, which caused her to follow her system religiously, allowed her little flexibility; that her style put a lid on her potential.

Ironically, Grace was a major risk taker in her personal life. When she moved out of her mother's house, she bought an old loft near Chicago's loop. Her tastes were spartan but striking; when she bought something it was unique and often expensive. Her purchases seemed designed to make a statement. She possessed an enlarged postcard of two lovers in a Budapest cafe; an unframed oil painting of a sleek leopard.

Her choice of male companions was also risky. Shunning bankers, money managers, and traders (who would frequently ask her out), she dated outrageous characters, including drug users and alcoholics, political radicals, and a variety of ne'er-do-wells. Grace was also sexually promiscuous.

On the job, Grace's discipline worked against her. She was unable to take creative risks. Her performance, though steady, was mediocre. Richard finally let her go from the trading team.

Grace was devastated. On the one hand, her self-image at work conformed to her mother's prescription—she was the epitome of stability and competence. On the other hand, her personal self-image was volatile and highly adventurous, one that invited danger.

Grace traded out of her self-image, rather than from her best interests. If she had been more flexible and viewed herself differently at work, things might have worked out. Like all of us, Grace juggled multiple perceptions of herself. The problem: She wasn't able to integrate those perceptions in a way that could meet her needs, both professionally and socially.

THE MASK OF THE COMPETITOR

The problem of split images is common. We all have multiple notions of who we are—some of them directly opposite from one another—but comforting to us in different situations. To ignore them in investing situations is dangerous, as is the belief that you can change an image overnight.

As our survey revealed, one of the masks investors reach for most often is that of the competitor. This mask is based on the myth of the successful investor as marketplace warrior, tremendously confident and bold as he defeats his enemies (bad trades) and comes away with the top prize. It's an attractive myth and supported by all the war stories about famous investors who fit the profile. The myth encourages putting on the mask and pushing away all those self-doubts and ambiguous feelings that hamper your ability to invest successfully.

You believe that you can be this person: the ruthless, arrogant, take-no-prisoners hero who, with a swashbuckling style, becomes a superstar investor. So you carefully put on your competitive mask and go for it.

Far more often than not, the mask fails to work its purported magic. At that point, when you find your losses mounting and your confidence crumbling, you may be ready to look at the person behind the mask.

LEARNING TO TRADE WITHIN YOURSELF

Years of events, important people, and experiences have shaped the internal images people have of themselves. You can't abandon a lifetime of image-shaping for a magical mask. To do this effectively, you would literally have to lose your mind; you would have to abandon everything you had become up to the point that you donned the mask.

Yes, you can push your internal images aside as you play at being Paul Tudor Jones. Yet you will always go home to yourself. Therefore, follow this advice: *If you can't beat you, then join you.*

Shelly S. learned this lesson the hard way.

Case Study

Shelly S. and Her False Self

Divorced with two children, Shelly was an astute shopper and saver. She probably spent half of what most women in her position did. Shelly worked as a data processing analyst for a major insurance company, making $40,000 a year. Her friends marveled at how she managed to save about $15,000 annually. Everyone told her she should learn about investing so she could turn her savings—almost $100,000—into an even larger sum, ensuring her children's security.

Though their advice made sense, Shelly wasn't a speculator or risk taker. But Shelly decided to explore this avenue, reading basic texts on the stock market and taking a 20-lesson home investing course. She learned about the business cycles, bond markets, inflation, commodities, stock market valuation, stock and commodity options, and fundamental and technical analysis.

Shelly opened a trading account at a local brokerage house and began to buy and sell stocks and stock options. Her performance was below average but not catastrophic. She decided she needed to learn more to become a better investor. She applied herself to learning technical analysis—moving averages, chart patterns, cycle and wave theories, stochastics. Shelly looked at various technical strategies, always set stops, and never risked more than 5 percent of her trading capital on any one trade.

Despite all she had learned, Shelly did poorly. Though she recognized she had to adopt a disciplined technical system and stick to it, she had trouble choosing one. She felt bad about herself; she couldn't shake the feeling of failure that accompanied her losses. But Shelly insisted to herself that she had to fail to succeed; that someone as bright and diligent as she was would succeed if she kept investing. Her friends' reinforced this viewpoint, encouraging her to keep plugging away.

Shelly tried. In the next few months, her investments continued to do poorly, and she had lost $50,000 of her $100,000 savings. Finally, she stopped investing; she focused on her job (at which she continued to do well) and managed to save $50,000 in the next three years. At that point, she wondered if she should start investing again. Then she met another programmer who was contemplating quitting his job and studying to be a financial consultant. He told Shelly about a course at the local college that offered a degree for certified financial planners. The program intrigued Shelly, and she enrolled in it, completing her certification while still working at the insurance company.

She ran an ad offering her services in the local paper, and she soon had a number of clients. Shelly was terrific at financial planning, and she acquired a sufficient number of clients to quit her job and devote herself full time to her new career. Her business thrived. Shelly found that her knack for saving combined with what she had learned about the financial markets ideally suited the requirements of her new job. Just as important, Shelly felt much more comfortable in her role as a saver rather than in her disguise as a speculator.

THE IMPORTANCE OF SHEDDING YOUR MASK

Shelly's problem, at least from an investing perspective, was extreme. She simply wasn't cut out to be a trader. She ignored her own positive self-image (as a saver) and tried to adopt an uncomfortable new self-image (as a speculator). The result: failure and a lowering of self-esteem.

Shelly succeeded when she recovered her self-image by saving $50,000; she then expanded and built on her self-image by gaining her certificate in financial planning, opening a financial planning business, and using the financial knowledge gained while trading. Shelly's self-esteem skyrocketed, along with her bank account.

The odds are that the mask you're wearing as an investor isn't as inappropriate to your self-image and to trading as Shelly's was. In her case, she was woefully unsuited to that activity. Unlike Shelly, you probably won't have to give up trading. But you should follow her example—shed your mask and capitalize on your positive self-image when trading.

THE "NEXT LEVEL UP" CONCEPT

The way to capitalize is by pinpointing your self-image and what you're good at; then apply those skills in a bigger arena where you can make more money. In a nutshell, this is the "next level up" concept.

For instance, you're a graphic artist at an ad agency and you're great at caricature drawings. If you put on the mask of the ambitious ad agency executive, you may be tempted to start your own ad agency to increase your income. But you probably don't have the skills or self-image to succeed in this endeavor. Perhaps you're introverted, and you're not particularly good at selling. Drop the mask and use your talent at caricature to draw a comic strip; recruit a copywriter down the hall who's great at creating funny dialogue; find an agent to represent you and sell your comic to a syndicate. This way, you're targeting the next level up.

A variation on this theme can involve combining disparate talents to move to a higher and more financially rewarding level. Let's say you're a decent trial lawyer with a major law firm. You're good but not great, and it's unlikely that you'll progress much in your career if you continue doing what you're doing. Quitting the law firm and starting your own won't work—you're not the type of superstar litigator that attracts clients. You analyze your talents and decide you've always been an excellent writer—as an undergraduate, you were a writer for the student newspaper and penned some well-received scripts for class plays. You decide to write a novel about one of your more sensational trials; or you apply to be a consultant for a prime-time television show about lawyers. For you, this combination of talents is a route to the next level up.

You can apply this concept to your investing. For example, you may have tried trading stock index options but have difficulty knowing when to sell. The premium erodes too rapidly for you. Yet, you have several positive self-image attributes working for you: You are excellent at grasping the exact stage of the business cycle; you are articulate and a good communicator, as well as an astute judge of character; you are also good at bringing people together toward common goals. Using the "next level up" concept, you might work closely with a trader who works with bond futures options. The two of you can work to bring a group of investors together in a limited partnership, earning a fee according to the performance of the trading system. Your grasp of the business cycle allows you to choose a trader of similar mind in an investment/trading vehicle geared toward your expertise. And, while the trader makes the buy/sell decisions, your people skills enable you to do well not only for the investors you enlist, but for yourself as well.

MASK AVOIDANCE—STAYING TRUE TO YOURSELF

It's easy to seize masks when investing. Even if you know it's wrong, you may be tempted. It's logical to model yourself after a highly successful trader or to be influenced by the idea of the trader as marketplace warrior.

Don't do it! To help you avoid these ill-fitting masks, keep the following four rules in mind:

1. *Identify Positive Investing/Trading Self-Images.* Make a list of the qualities that define you as a person, including the strengths and talents that experience has demonstrated you possess (not ones that you wish you had).

2. *Avoid Uncomfortable Strategies or Arenas That Don't Build on Your Positive Self-Images.* If you're a spontaneous, instinctive person, don't force yourself to adhere to a highly technical trading strategy that locks you into a model.

3. *Don't Lie to Yourself About What You Believe In.* This characteristic will be discussed in the next section of this chapter.

4. *Take New Risks within the Sphere of Your Positive Self-Image—Don't Stagnate.* In other words, don't allow yourself to get in an investing rut, following the same "script" day in and day out, fearful that you "don't have what it takes." One appropriate way to take risks is through the "next level up" concept.

MATCHING YOUR BELIEFS AND
YOUR INVESTING

Think about what you really believe in. If your investing runs counter to those beliefs, the contradiction will diminish your investing ability. What are your values? If you strongly believe that apartheid is wrong, you shouldn't invest in companies that do business with South Africa. If you persist in such investments, it's likely that you'll punish yourself for it. One way or another, you'll create an investment strategy that will reprimand you for investing in companies that violate your values.

Similarly, define your ideals. If your ideal world is one of peace with a government that focuses on social ills rather than defense spending, don't try to make money on defense stocks. In addition, don't try to play games with your ideals when investing. You may try to short a stock or option that is at odds with your ideals, assuming this approach will keep your ideals intact. It won't. Making money on the downside still capitalizes on the existence of an institution that doesn't have a place in your ideals. You'll be fighting yourself, and you're bound to lose the fight.

Conversely, if in your heart you believe that "rugged individualism" is good—that people must learn how to take responsibility for their own lives—then you can't successfully wear a "take care of others" mask while investing. You might want to look like Mr. Nice Guy, but you will suffer financially. Companies that provide lifetime employment or who reward employees for seniority won't work for you. Firms that are supposed to profit from drug rehabilitation programs won't fit in with what you really believe.

Finally, model yourself after an investor whose approach you endorse from both strategic and ethical perspectives. Don't eliminate the hero-investor's values and ideals from the equation. If the methods of your model strike you as underhanded in any way, you will not be able to use them successfully. When you buy into someone else's methods, you buy into every aspect of those methods. If some aspect goes against the grain of your beliefs, you won't be able to discount it—at least, your unconscious won't, no matter how much your conscious self wants to.

THE GRANDIOSE MASK

For investors who fall in this category, grandiosity is a powerful yet subtle danger. It arises from a sense of destiny and greatness, an attractive mask that hides inferiority feelings. If you could journey to an investors' graveyard (or, perhaps more appropriately, bankruptcy court), you would find tombstones of people who were victims of their own enlarged sense of themselves.

They felt they could do no wrong. If one trade doesn't pan out, the next one will. The grandiose investor can't conceive failure and ignores the risks.

Like most things, grandiosity is okay in moderation. It provides investors with sufficient confidence to take the risks inherent in virtually every trading scenario. But when grandiosity becomes excessive, it also becomes fatal. You start to ignore all risks, driven by the certainty that you're always going to come out on top. You lose perspective and, worse, lose touch with who you really are.

"MY KINGDOM FOR MORE CAPITAL"— THE RICHARD III SYNDROME

A variation on the preceding theme: Your money manager rather than you wears the grandiose mask. Remember Richard III, Shakespeare's messianic ruler who had the shriveled arm? More instructively, you might recall the Monty Python spoof of this tragic hero: His arms and legs were cut off, but he proclaimed that "it's only a scratch" and there was no way he was going to lose the battle.

The grandiose money manager is charismatic. If you feel inferior, you can banish that feeling by glomming onto your money manager's grandiosity. He or she has the "power," and your association will allow you to share in it.

No question, money managers who wear such masks have legions of true believers. Regardless of their actual performance, they create the illusion that they are market wizards. They can convince anyone that they can squeeze water from a stone—or that they can steer you to investments with great rewards and no risks.

Whether you're entrusting your investing to someone who wears this mask or you're wearing it yourself, recognize that you must look underneath for your trading to be successful. Strip away the grandiosity and look at the record: The numbers don't lie. Don't let yourself believe that a series of setbacks are temporary, that you have to have unwavering faith in your ability (or your money manager's ability) to win in the end. No matter how wonderful that grandiose mask feels—and it does feel wonderful—the mask is only temporary. The harsh reality of continued big losses dissolves it, and then it's too late to do anything.

When you start to think you're an invulnerable investor or that your money manager is a financial Superman, take a step back and look in the mirror. If you see a mask, take it off immediately and get back to reality.

ACTION PLAN FOR THE MASKED INVESTOR

The following action plan is designed to help you invest, based on who you are rather than who you think you should be. Adhering to these steps will enable you to translate your strengths as a person into investing scenarios, free from confining and competing investing personalities.

1. *Be Who You Are.* As the wise old Greek advised, "Know thyself, and to thine own self be true." Analyze your personality during those moments when you're making a trade. Do you see a stranger? If so, try and adopt a more familiar persona.

2. *Don't Create a New Image.* If you have some idealized image of yourself as investor—an image that bears no resemblance to who you are when you're at work or with friends and family—discard it.

3. *Identify What You're Good at and How These Strengths Might Serve You Relative to Investing.* Make a list of your major strengths: an analytical mind, the ability to think on your feet, perceptivity about trends, and so on. Are you capitalizing on these strengths when you invest?

4. *Pinpoint Subsidiary Talents.* What are your "second-tier" strengths? Perhaps they're underdeveloped or neglected talents. They might be abilities that your current job doesn't capitalize on, but that you've used earlier in your life.

5. *Consider How You Can Combine Your Primary and Subsidiary Talents and Use That Combination to Move to the Next Level Up.* Is there an investing approach that will best serve this combination? Spend a lot of time with this concept. Go back in this chapter and review it. There is a great potential for success in it.

6. *Think about What's Really Important to You.* Identify your values: what you think is right and wrong. Determine if your investments are consistent with your values. If not, think about ways to change your investing strategy to make them consistent.

7. *Figure Out What Your Ideals Are.* One way to do this is to create a scenario for your perfect investment. Is your trading/investing in line with this perfect investment? If not, how can you create a better alignment?

8. *Think about the Person Who Serves as Your Investing Model.* Are his or her values and ideals consistent with yours? Are you uncomfortable with your model's methods from ethical or moral standpoints? If not, you should find another model.

9. *Determine Your Tendency for Feelings of Grandiosity and Inferiority.* Examine five recent trades you made, and decide if such feelings were present. Resolve to find a middle ground between the two during your next trade, refusing to give in to the "I can do no wrong" trap.

10. *Don't Get Caught up in a Money Manager's Grandiosity.* One exercise to help you do this is to write down your manager's strengths: What abilities does he or she really possess when it comes to handling your investments? Then make a parallel list of what attracts you to this particular money manager. If you find the first list is woefully brief and the second one is filled with adjectives such as "charisma," "confidence," and "exciting ideas," then you might want to find a manager who has more substance than style.

   After having hopped on the fast train bound for glory, if you don't have confidence in the scope of your broker's abilities, you'd best get off at the next safe stop. Remember, there will always be another train, and this will give you time to see what the real "track" record has been. Inspect the train, the tracks, and the route carefully. It is better to get where you want to go safely, even it it takes a little longer. The grandiose mask you wear may be impeding your vision.

CHAPTER 13

The Fussy Investor

Remember the Tony Randall character, Felix Ungar, from television's *The Odd Couple?* Felix couldn't stand to see a speck of dust on the floor or a hair out of place on his head. He was galled by any hint of disorder. If a picture hung on a wall was even slightly crooked, he'd be compelled to straighten it.

Imagine Felix Ungar as an investor and you have this chapter's profile. Apply adjectives such as obsessive, compulsive, and orderly and you'll get a sense of the fussy investor.

Our survey showed that many of you fall into this category. But it also revealed: If you're only moderately fussy, it won't negatively affect your investing; if you're overly fussy, however, this trait will significantly decrease your chances for success.

Case Study

Mark W., A Mildly Fussy Investor

Mark W. is a 36-year-old, married man who responded in our survey of part-time investors. He considers himself to be a successful trader. He answers "7" (on a scale of 0–7 points) to the following statements:

- I stick with my system no matter what the loss.
- I am a very orderly person.
- I am a content person.
- I calculate the risk/loss of each potential trade or investment.

In his comments section, Mark revealed that he sees himself as someone who has a definite plan and executes it precisely. In addition, he mentioned that it is important to him to have his work done ahead of time.

Mark is a "fussy" investor. He wants things done right—and right away. He gets irritated if things aren't done properly. Yet, Mark is only mildly "fussy." In fact, being mildly fussy has worked to his advantage, for he often enjoys success in his trading.

Case Study

Martin Y., An Overly Fussy Investor

On the other hand, Martin Y., a 48-year-old married man who responded to our part-time trader survey, noted that he is not a very successful trader. His survey results were interesting for several reasons. Let's take a look at his responses and comments.

Martin answered 6 or 7 (strongly positive) to the following statements:

- Frequently, unwanted thoughts about my trades/investments come into my mind.
- I stick with my system, no matter what the loss.
- I am a very orderly person.
- I am aware of the specific profit I can make from a trade/investment.
- Trading/investing has interfered with my work life.
- Trading/investing has interfered with my social life.
- I calculate out the risk/loss of each potential trade/investment.

In his comments section, Martin reported that he worries and frets a lot, and that he hides his emotions and doesn't communicate well. Martin said that, in his free time, he enjoys fixing things, but only when the project comes out perfectly.

While Mark W. is a *"mildly* fussy" trader, Martin is an *"overly* fussy" trader—a style that is detrimental to his success as a trader. Whereas Mark benefits from a little bit of fussiness, Martin's need for extreme precision and order gets in the way of his better judgment and interferes with his success.

Now, let's determine if the fussy moniker applies to you.

TEST YOUR FUSSINESS QUOTIENT

Answer the following questions *yes* or *no:*

- Do you constantly change your mind about investments or trades?
- Do you have trouble acting decisively when buying or selling?
- Do you hold onto old records or certificates when they clearly have no real or even sentimental value?
- Are you so perfectionistic in your research about a trade or investment that you end up not doing it?
- Do you insist that your broker or partners do trades or deals in exactly the manner you prescribe?
- Are you scrupulous to the extent that few can live up to your standards for investing or trading?
- Are you frequently less generous than you might be?
- Do you need to be much more emotionally expressive?
- Are you so involved with trading/investing that you've left little time for friends and family?

If you've answered *yes* to less than five of these questions, than you probably don't fit this investor type. If your *yes* responses total five or six, you're on a potentially dangerous borderline. More than six and you're overly fussy.

As we've mentioned, a moderate degree of fussiness probably won't hurt your investing. But if you have a tendency toward fussiness, you can easily slip into a Felix Ungar-like state. Or, more precisely, you can become an obsessive investor like Steve.

Case Study

Steve B. and His Treasured Charts

A 52-year-old retired architect, Steve B. decided to make the commodity markets his second career. Though he'd been successful in his first career, it was marked by constant run-ins with the draftspeople who worked for him. He always felt their work was not sufficiently precise. Frequently, he revised their drawings. Steve's partners didn't object to these revisions since they were always perfect.

Steve had meticulously studied the futures markets on retirement, and he decided that he would trade in three commodities: silver, T-bonds and the major market index. He assumed he could capitalize on whatever movements were taking place regardless of the business cycle phase.

It took Steve six months to decide that he would trade in these three markets, and he spent another three months picking out a brokerage house to place his orders. He issued specific requirements to the house, setting time frames for how long he'd give them to answer his phone calls; take, execute, and confirm his orders; and send him confirmation slips in the mail.

Though Steve had a computer, he decided to do his charting by hand. He used a compass, a ruler and colored pencils to create picture-perfect charts. In these charts, he included relative strength, stochastics, moving averages, and figure charts. He spent three hours each evening updating his charts for the three markets. Because he started charting immediately after the markets closed, he had little time to spend with his wife—he couldn't even eat dinner with her. When his wife insisted he refrain from charting so they could do something together, he became extremely anxious and irritable.

While Steve found his charting activity to be a great relief from the hectic market turmoil during the day, he was waking up in the middle of the night worried that he had missed something or made a mistake; he'd jump out of bed to check his charts. He knew this behavior was excessive and even admitted it to his wife, but he said he couldn't help himself.

Ironically, Steve rarely executed a trade. On average, he made two trades every six months. Usually, they were losing trades. Steve would agonize about whether to hold a position and rarely did. Though he didn't lose a lot of money, he also didn't show a profit during his first three years of trading.

FROM FUSSY TO OBSESSIVE

Steve is an extreme example of this investor type. But one step below Steve is a significantly large number of investors with enough obsessive-compulsive characteristics to prevent them from ever coming out ahead.

There's a fine line between the diligent, detail-oriented investor and the one who studies a trade to death. When you cross that line, you're in trouble. You lose sight of your goal—to make money. Instead, you become tangled in the process leading to the goal: You get so caught up in the nitty-gritty details that your efforts become counterproductive.

You lose your ability to be decisive.

You become a reactive rather than a proactive trader.

You delude yourself into thinking you're being thorough while in reality you're being fussy.

Successful investors strike a balance between thought and action, between research and intuition. At some point, they have to shove their intellectual activity aside and move. As the old saying goes, he who hesitates is lost.

Overly fussy investors hesitate, procrastinate, and lose themselves in too much debate. Like Felix Ungar eyeing the crooked picture on the wall, they straighten and restraighten their trading strategy to the point that it's never going to "hang" properly. It's not the picture that's crooked but the way they're looking at it.

Are you an overly fussy investor? Based on our research, we've created a snapshot of this person's cluttered mind as it might appear during the trading process. See if it matches up with what's going on inside your head.

PORTRAIT OF THE FUSSY INVESTOR

Your trades hover in your mind, bothering you. It's an intrusive sensation. You try (and fail) to ignore these intrusive thoughts about your positions, broker, charts, and real estate.

Your thoughts make you so tense that you try to do something, anything, to decrease that anxiety—calling your broker, rechecking your charts, rechecking your balance, rereading a newspaper article about a company in which you're trading.

You believe that by rechecking, recalling, and rereading, you can prevent something bad from happening to your investments.

You realize your behavior is excessive.

The preceding activities take up more than an hour daily; they may also interfere with your job, your social life, your preinvestment routine.

Overly fussy investors can manifest different "symptoms"; they may suffer from "obsessive-compulsive" disorder. The following three are the most common:

- *Checking.* You can't stop thinking about or checking your trades. It becomes a ritual that you practice constantly. Your mind replays the details of a trade, not just once, but many times. Or you check the price of a stock in the paper five times a day, as if you may have not got it right the first time, and some magical editor is revising the price between checks.

- *Washing.* You feel dirty or infected. In a noninvestment scenario, this symptom may literally involve frequent handwashing. As an investor, you may find yourself cleaning your computer screen with a numbing regularity. Or you're certain that a virus has infected your software and you futilely try to find the bug. Or it might be the unfounded suspicion that your broker is cheating you; that he or she is churning your account—you start asking leading questions designed to assess the broker's honesty.

- *Hoarding.* You collect and save every scrap of paper related to your trades. This symptom goes beyond creating an investment library. You can't throw anything out. You've accumulated so many newsletters, magazines, and charts that this paper trail is taking over your living space. It's as if each document takes on a perceived value that prohibits you from disposing of it; you irrationally believe that a three-year-old copy of a defunct newsletter may come in handy someday.

The fussy investor not only exhibits different symptoms but can be plagued by various trading errors. Let's look at two fussy investors who are light years removed (in terms of their personalities) from Steve, but who are thwarted in their trading by two distinct aspects of the fussy syndrome.

Case Study

What Is Sally Missing?

Sally H. left her PhD economics program at New York University to trade crude oil futures at the New York Mercantile Exchange. Sally was energetic and outgoing; she was everyone's friend. But her personality tended to go up and down with the market. When it took a nosedive, she became dramatically distraught. When it went up, she was on a high. Most of her fellow traders in the pit liked her a lot. Her social life was active, though men with whom she developed relationships found her somewhat vain and demanding.

Recently, Sally lost some money on two moderate-sized trades and began to doubt her trading system. Although she was still ahead by 40 percent for the year, the doubts caused her to ask herself, "What am I missing?"

Her system was still functioning reasonably well—her next two trades were successful. But the doubts wouldn't go away. She'd wake up at night and try to confront her doubts, checking the data she collected, her entry and exit parameters. On the surface, nothing seemed amiss. Yet a little voice in her head kept whispering, "You're missing something."

That voice caused her to hold back on several entry points and she missed out on the massive bull market just after Iraq's invasion of Kuwait. Ironically, it turned out that she was missing something else—the thousands of dollars she might have made if she had stuck to her system and ignored that fussy little voice.

Case Study

Fred's Need for Control

Fred J. was driving his broker crazy. Tom, the broker, received calls from Fred four or five times each day. He tried to tell Fred that the daily calls had to stop, but it was difficult. Fred was a nice guy, and he apologized profusely to Tom for being such a bother. So Tom tolerated Fred's calls, as well as his bizarre, step-by-step instructions on how to make a trade and his frantic calls to "turn on your computer and fill me in on the latest quotes."

As a child, Fred had been the victim of a tyrannical father. He was beaten by his father for any behavior that didn't please him. Mistakes were not allowed when he was growing up. His father didn't tolerate errors. So Fred worried constantly, in terrible fear of physical and emotional punishment.

As an adult, Fred took a careful and perfectionist approach to his life. He paid such intense attention to every task that his friends sometimes thought he was crazy; they couldn't understand why he always needed to know everything possible about a movie or play before agreeing to see it. At the same time, everyone liked Fred. He was extraordinarily considerate of other people's feelings; he would never do unto others as his father had done to him. When he realized his controlling attitude was rubbing others the wrong way, he would profusely apologize.

Fred's insistence on control in investing scenarios was detrimental to his success. He refused to accept that an investment can never be totally controlled; that there's an element of chance that

you have to live with and adjust to if you're going
to be successful.

ACTION PLAN FOR THE FUSSY INVESTOR

If you suspect that you're a fussy investor, the following
four steps will help you avoid the negatives of your
"type" and capitalize on the positives.

1. *Assemble Helpful People.* In many instances, this
means finding a broker or other financial advisor who
can moderate the mistakes you make because of your
fussiness. According to our survey, many professional
traders consider "using helpful people" to be a key psychological tool for success. Sally needed someone to help
her understand that she wasn't "missing something"; to
assuage her crippling doubts. Fred needed someone to
keep his obsession for control under control.

Luckily, his broker, Tom, was that someone. Tom set
limits for Fred. Tom explained that if Fred didn't place
an order within the first minute of the phone call, he
would hang up. He would allow Fred a maximum of five
phone calls per week. He promised that he would call
Fred within an hour after an order was filled and tell
him the prices—this phone call, too, would be limited to
one minute.

Tom's approach brought success, from both a psychological and a trading standpoint. Tom's firm but friendly
limits made sense to Fred. He helped Fred realize that
his controlling impulses were detrimental to his trading;
that limits were necessary and would increase his odds of
success.

In a way, Fred's broker was substituting a reasonable
control system for an unreasonable one.

Your financial advisor or broker should be able to reg-
ulate the worst aspects of your fussy tendencies. Don't

assume any broker will fit the bill. Some will simply bow to your will, allowing your fussiness full reign. Others will be intolerable—you won't be able to work with them because they treat you like the fussy child they perceive you to be. It's not unusual for fussy investors to be "fired" by broker after broker who can't tolerate their unreasonable demands.

Tom was the ideal broker for Fred. Once you understand your particular brand of fussiness, look for the broker who is best suited to deal with that aspect of your investing personality.

2. *Loosen Up.* To paraphrase the lyrics of Stevie Wonder, fussy investors are uptight and their feelings are out of sight. Use and study your mind/money journal and construct a personal money timeline to find a way out of the narrow little world you inhabit. Determine why you're so perfectionistic and how it's affecting your investing. Have you always been this way? Do certain events and situations worsen the condition? What good trades and investments have you missed because of your obsessive tendencies?

Experiment with being a bit looser. Take small steps at first. Try to make a trade and refuse to recheck every available piece of data before you make it. Make a small trade based on your gut feelings about a stock rather than reams of research. Once you try these things a few times, it might break the logjam of obsessiveness. Once you see that there are no horrible repercussions to being a tad less fussy, you'll find it easier to loosen up.

3. *Find an Outlet for Your Fussy Feelings.* This outlet might be psychotherapy. Whether you're a checker, a washer, or a hoarder, whether you feel as if you're missing something or you need tight control, whether you're obsessive, compulsive, or all of the above, you should talk about it with a professional. Talking isn't a panacea, but it might help you put your fussy feelings in perspective and allow you to segregate them from the

investing marketplace. Rather than placing a series of self-defeating shackles on your broker, it's better to tell someone about why you feel you need to use those shackles. Just talking about it may be therapeutic. You might realize that you're being overly fussy, and it might moderate your fussy investment behavior. And, you may learn a few valuable, strategic tools to help you deal with your obsessions and compulsions.

If your condition is so severe that it permeates almost every aspect of your life, there are new medications that may help you. If you think your situation may require drug therapy, please consult a psychiatrist.

4. *Recognize the Advantages and Disadvantages of Your Fussy Tendencies.* There are advantages. Professional investor Marty Zweig claims he's always worried about everything and never feels that he's done all his homework. He uses an enormous number of indicators and is constantly fussing over which one is working best. His investing record is terrific, so obviously his obsessiveness works for him. Your perfectionistic inclinations can also work for you. Making sure all the *t*'s are crossed and all the *i*'s are dotted can help you avoid the errors that plague less detail-oriented investors. Just don't let all the *t*-crossing and *i*-dotting become the main ingredients of your investing strategy. It can drain your energy, create indecision, and shift your focus away from more important investing matters.

Keep a balance. Though you don't want to be like Felix Ungar, you also don't want to become Oscar Madison. Sloppy investors are no better off than fussy ones (they're probably worse off). As an overly fussy investor, however, you're missing the creativity and instincts of someone like Oscar. You can move in that direction without creating massive disorder in your investment house.

CHAPTER 14

The Paranoid Investor

I f my broker would have acted sooner, I would have made a killing."

"My system is going to be the death of me; I should have junked it a long time ago."

"If the charts were posted on time, I wouldn't have made that blunder."

The preceding comments are typical of the paranoid investor, as is the attitude, "It's somebody else's fault."

No question, the investing marketplace breeds a certain amount of paranoia in all of us. When your ego is tied up with your investing, it's easy to blame someone else for your mistakes or to assign fault to explain inexplicable turns in the market. To a certain extent, all investors are paranoid. But when paranoia becomes the dominant factor in your investing, watch out! You start looking over your shoulder every step of the way, and you take your eye off the investing ball. Your energy is devoted to finding scapegoats and assigning blame, rather than to making wise investment decisions.

As a truly paranoid investor, you don't trust yourself and you don't trust the advice of others—or, as we'll explain a little later in this chapter, you experience the paranoid backlash of trusting someone too much. You treat everything you read and hear with suspicion. Every valuable nugget of information that crosses your desk is perceived as fool's gold.

Do you fit into the paranoid cluster? Look over the following list of traits and see how many apply to you.

PROFILE OF THE PARANOID INVESTOR

- Doesn't trust his or her own instincts.
- Feels an intense need for a guru or mentor.
- Blames "outside" people and factors for bad investments.
- Has trouble handling compliments; feels embarrassed or disbelieving when complimented.
- Has bad relationship with same-sex parent.
- Willing to risk everything on one roll of the investment dice.

Does this sound like you? To confirm your suspicions, determine if you bear a resemblance to the following paranoid investor.

Case Study

Sally V., Stranded by a System

A 33-year-old New Jersey housewife, Sally V. is married to Donald, a successful advertising executive. Sally had always been in charge of the family's finances, and about a year ago she decided that they should invest a portion of their considerable savings in stocks.

After learning about growth stocks and contacting a brokerage house that specialized in these securities, Sally decided to invest $30,000. Sally met with her broker, Sarah, who helped her learn about the market and small capitalization stocks. The more Sally learned about these stocks, the more excited she got; she couldn't wait to start trading.

Sally visited Sarah in her office to see how a brokerage house worked and was impressed with Sarah's office and other indications of her success. After warning Sally about stock trading commission costs and risks, Sarah helped Sally find two stocks: one for a small microchip company and another for a small biotech firm. They followed the trading pattern of these equities and established their current "box"—the support and resistance levels they were trading between. They determined that they would buy when the stock hit a certain support level and sell when it hit the resistance point.

Sally began trading two biotech stocks. One made a new drug for treatment of AIDS patients and the other a drug for depression. Both had made sharp moves up and down in the past. Sarah plotted their support and resistance levels for Sally, and both stocks hit their resistance levels almost simultaneously. Per Sarah's instructions, Sally sold both and set her stops at 13% above the resistance price. The AIDS stock broke through resistance by about 8% but then plummeted back down into the trading range. When it was about 10% above the support level, Sally bought it back, again according to Sarah's instructions.

The depression drug stock solidly broke through the resistance level and Sally got stopped out. It established a new trading range.

Sally wasn't disappointed; she'd actually made a little bit of money on the AIDS stock, yet most of the gain evaporated when commissions and taxes were taken out. Still, Sarah suggested they stick with their game plan.

Sarah and Sally talked on the phone quite a bit. Sally felt close to Sarah; she found herself talking not only about her stocks, but about her personal life. Soon, she began to view Sarah as more than her broker—she considered Sarah one of her best friends.

Then Sally sold the depression drug stock short when it hit its new resistance level. It dropped, but only about 10%, then hovered around resistance level before it broke through to the upside and Sally got stopped out again.

This time, Sally was upset. Secretly, she blamed Sarah. "She puts so much faith in her system," she fumed and cynically noted, "She acts like her system is foolproof, when obviously it's not."

A few weeks later, the AIDS stock got close to support and Sally bought it, still sticking with Sarah's game plan. She was bullish on the stock, wanting to buy more, but such a move wouldn't have been in keeping with Sarah's strategy. The depression drug stock, however, bothered her. When it finally broke down back through support, Sally wanted to short it because she felt that it was going to enter the old trading range. Sarah, however, said that it hadn't broken down more than 10% through the support level and technically, they should be buying it. They did neither.

It turned out that Sally was right: The depression stock entered the old trading trading range and ran down to its old support level. If she had followed her instincts, she would have made a nice profit.

Over the next year, Sally felt increasingly frustrated with her trading. She resisted her impulse to short the depression stock at the resistance level and buy the AIDS stock at its support level. Instead, she stuck with Sarah's system and lost $4500 after six months. After another six months and an additional $4000 in losses, Sally stopped trading.

PARANOIA AND THE DEPENDENCY PITFALL

Sally trusted Sarah and her system completely. As a paranoid investor, how could Sally trust anyone? Because paranoid investors have so little self-trust and self-confidence, they reach out in desperation to find someone who will provide what they lack. They embrace mentors, gurus, and others with a passion. Like Sally, they fail to pay attention to or act on their own knowledge, instincts, and observations.

The Epstein–Garfield survey puts this point into a startling perspective. Of all those surveyed who were in the "successful" category, half had mentors. In and of itself, there's nothing particularly revealing about that statistic. However, not one of the paranoid investor respondents who were successful had mentors!

From investing and psychological perspectives, this finding makes eminent sense. Paranoid individuals often have excellent instincts; they simply don't trust those instincts. They look for substitutes—people or things who, they assume, possess greater wisdom and insight than they do.

If you are a paranoid investor, these substitutes don't suffice. Inevitably, you'll begin to distrust your mentor or broker. Like Sally, you'll resent the broker's control and question his or her competence or motives when things go poorly. At the same time, you'll be afraid to question or criticize your broker—you're so dependent on the relationship, you can't bring yourself to do anything that might disturb it.

Another problem: No broker, mentor, system, or newsletter is foolproof. Brokers, particularly, require input from clients. When you don't provide a broker with input—when you don't give your broker the benefit of your observations, feelings, and knowledge—you're doing both yourself and your broker a disservice. Like Sally, you're setting yourself up for a fall. In many instances, you might not recover sufficiently to trade again. We've seen numerous examples of paranoid investors who suffer losses and vow never to invest again—the market, after all, is out to get them, and they're not going to be played for a sucker twice.

Such thinking is obviously wrong. The market isn't out to get you, if you are a paranoid investor; you're out to get yourself. You lack the internal fortitude to trust yourself in investing scenarios.

For now, keep this point in mind: If you're a paranoid investor, the worst possible thing you can do is to become totally dependent on another person for your investing success.

GOING FOR BROKE

At some point in their investing lives, paranoid investors often take a big gamble. It's not a calculated gamble; it's one that's impulsive and often self-destructive.

Again, this might seem at odds with the common perception of paranoia. If you're paranoid, doesn't that mean you never take big gambles; that you're too distrustful of everything and everyone to take a big risk?

Though that analysis makes surface sense, in reality paranoid investors take unhealthy risks in a quest for the "big score" that will solve all their problems. They're looking for a miracle cure for their paranoia, for the suspicion and distrust that dogs them. Because paranoid investors harbor the fear that it's all going to be taken away from them anyway, why not go out with a bang rather than a whimper? Why not go out in a heroic burst of investing bravado rather than getting nickel and dimed to death?

Here's a typical scenario. A paranoid investor sees the market in a downdraft and decides to go along. He risks far more than normal on 10 index future contracts; before, he'd never traded more than two. Why is he doing it now when he's never done such a thing before? His actions are not the result of detailed analysis, inside information, or a gut feeling that this is a once-in-a-lifetime opportunity. More likely, his gamble is the result of years of paranoia, of small losses and small wins and a conviction that if he continues the same investing strategy he'll never win big. So he cavalierly throws caution to the wind and bets a bundle.

The odds are that he'll lose. He's letting his paranoia dictate his trading, and the result will be that after he loses his bet, he'll be even more convinced that the market was out of get him and it got him in a big way.

PULLING BACK WHEN YOU SHOULD PUSH FORWARD

The third mind-over-money obstacle facing the paranoid investor is a lack of conviction. Time and again, we've seen people in this cluster refuse to commit themselves to sound strategies. They've achieved a moderate amount of investing success—whatever they're doing is working. It's logical that they continue with their approach or even invest more; no big losses or new market conditions suggest that they should change.

And yet they do. Their paranoia creeps up on them and says, "You're gonna lose. Your strategy is going to turn against you; you're a sucker if you think you can continue on the same course; you're just being set up for a fall." They react by junking their strategy; or by going in an opposite direction; or by refusing to invest in vehicles that have worked for them in the past.

To the outside observer, such a reaction seems insane. But to the paranoid investor, it makes perfect sense.

Barry, who traded Japanese yen, was a victim of this type of paranoid thinking. Let's look at how he was victimized, and how he worked through the problem.

Case Study

Barry's Yen

Barry D., a divorced 49-year-old liquor store owner, followed the Japanese yen like a hawk. Fascinated by Japan's growing domination of various markets, he was convinced the yen would supersede the dollar just as the dollar had once overtaken the British pound sterling. Barry studied international interest rates, trade balances, and political events. He was a student of the business cycle in both the United States and Japan. An avid believer in cycles and trading systems based on cycles, Barry traded five contracts of the Japanese yen. Though he came out a little ahead after a period of trading, he always seemed to pull out too soon, unable to stay with a trend long enough to make a significant profit.

Barry's relationship with his wife was a clue to his problem. Though Stephanie, his wife, considered him to be a nice guy and hard worker, she complained that there was no intimacy in their relationship, that their sexual relationship was mechanical, and that he didn't want to get "close." When Stephanie confronted Barry with her feelings, Barry responded that the problem was his worries about foreign currency markets. Stephanie grew increasingly irritated with her husband, especially his inability to trust her or communicate his deepest feelings. Eventually, she filed for divorce.

Barry's approach to yen trading was not much different from his approach to Stephanie; he never was close enough to the market. It wasn't that he traded too many or too few contracts; it was that he pulled the plug too soon. He couldn't seem to stay with a move. He'd rationalize that he made a bit of a profit, and then he'd get out before the market turned on him. It just wasn't in him to stay with a cycle, to see his strategy through. As a result, his trading record was mediocre. If his yen strategy could have taken on human form, it too would have been fed up and divorced him.

Barry started seeing a therapist. During therapy sessions, Barry learned a bit about his problem with paranoia. By talking with the therapist, he received a picture of how he seemed to others: his lack of trust, his inability to embrace anything or anyone wholeheartedly.

It wasn't anything magical or instantaneous, but the sessions helped Barry become more aware of his problem. Just talking about it seemed to help.

For that reason, he made a lunch date with someone he knew who also traded yen futures. They discussed foreign interest rates and technical aspects of trading. From their talk, it was obvious this investor had made a fortune from his trading; it was instructive to hear him explain how many contracts he traded, how often, his average profit per trade.

After lunching with his new friend a few times, and about 10 weeks into therapy, Barry decided to make some adjustments in his trading: He would let his profits run 10 percent longer than he had in the past. Barry viewed the adjustments as a temporary experiment. He would give his strategy three months.

During those three months, his profits improved significantly. More valuable than the money was the lesson he learned that he could risk a little more—and trust his strategy a little more—and he wouldn't get hurt. Slowly but surely, Barry was able to keep his paranoia at bay and away from his investment strategy.

ACTION PLAN FOR THE PARANOID INVESTOR

What should you do if you're confronted with the paranoid investor's obstacles to success? We've designed the following five-step plan to overcome the common obstacles:

1. *Reject Extreme Investing Behavior.* Paranoid investors are tempted by extremes. They cede all responsibility for their investing decisions to a broker, guru, or mentor; they're willing to risk everything on one roll of the dice; they're suspicious of everything and everyone (except the person they put too much trust in). Use your mind/money journal to find examples of extreme investing behavior. Ask yourself if these examples have hurt or limited your investing success. If so, put a temporary halt to these extreme actions. If it means ending a relationship with a trusted broker or junking a treasured system, do it!

2. *Practice Moderation.* Experiment with less extreme investing strategies. Instead of placing all your trust in one person, develop a group of advisors—friends,

other traders, and so on. Use this group as a sounding board for your investment decisions. Also, try to give a newsletter, investing system, or other information source the benefit of the doubt. Make a small investment based on the source's information and see what happens.

3. *Trust Your Instincts.* Make a few, low-risk investments based on how you feel about a particular trade. Ignore everything but your gut feelings. Look to your dreams and fantasies for clues to those gut feelings.

4. *Take the Next, Logical Step.* Add to positions, trade more frequently when you're winning, stay with winners longer, keep cutting back on losers if that's working. Above all else, don't pull back because of some vague, unsubstantiated fear that everything's going to come crashing down. Slowly but surely, build on your successful strategy. Don't let a small downturn in your investment performance cause you to fold your tent. Pace yourself and take moderate breaks from trading. Stick with what's been working.

5. *When Things Go Wrong, Find Out the Real Why.* Paranoid investors react to setbacks with hand-wringing anxiety. They assign blame to convenient scapegoats: their advisors, their systems. Take the time to investigate the real source of a loss. Using your personal and family money timeline, check to see if you may have inherited this "overly cautious" approach. Talk to friends and investment professionals; read as much as you can; find someone else who suffered similar losses. The more you investigate, the less likely you are to automatically blame your "straw men." Sometimes, the loss was due to a blunder on your part or bad advice. More often, the cause was isolated, correctable, or beyond your control. Once you begin to unearth the real reasons behind losses, you won't rely on fictitious, paranoid reasons to explain them. More importantly, you won't pull back from your investing strategy because you assume that your judgment is inadequate.

Underlying all five steps of the action plan is the concept of trust—or, more to the point, distrust. Paranoid investors not only distrust others, they distrust themselves. From an investment standpoint, the consequence of this distrust is to view brokers, systems, newsletters, and virtually every piece of information with a rejecting eye. At times, paranoid investors react to their negative self-image by doing a 180-degree turn; they blindly trust a broker or a particular investment that really is unworthy of total trust.

The five steps of the action plan should help you reconstruct your approach to trust. By doing so, you'll be able to invest with more confidence in yourself and others, and you'll be able to analyze the advice you receive perceptively and objectively.

CHAPTER 15

The Wild Card Types

Our survey of nonprofessional traders and investors revealed six psychological clusters or types of investors. What it didn't reveal is what we refer to as the "wild card" types—not quite as common as our six clusters, but still likely to pop up. Specifically, we've encountered the following two psychological types in our professional practices: the "addicted" investor and the "sociopathic" investor. You should be aware of the former and beware of the latter. Many of us, though we may not be truly addicted investors, have traits of the addict and, therefore, should be keenly aware of the challenges these traits may pose to our investing.

The sociopathic investor/trader is far less common but can do a great deal of damage to us; we should learn how to spot this destructive type and prevent him or her from influencing our investment decisions.

THE ADDICTED INVESTOR

Many people use investing as a disguise. They're hooked and they don't know it. Unlike the guy who makes frequent junkets to Vegas and admits he's a compulsive gambler, addicted investors would be shocked if you pinned that label on them. They prefer to call themselves frequent traders rather than compulsive gamblers.

Inside every addicted investor's brain is a plea for Lady Luck to be on his side. Like the Vegas visitor, there's an unconscious appeal to some mysterious power to help put the bet on the winning number. While other investor types might place their faith in themselves, their systems, or their brokers, the addicted investor pays homage to Lady Luck.

Out of Control

All addictions involve a loss of control. Addicts, however, often fool themselves into believing that they have a handle on the situation. They are under the illusion that they are willfully calling all the shots—placing the orders or selling the stock, for instance. In truth, however, they are out of control.

You can compare this addiction to any drug addiction. Addicted investors feel immediate gratification when they are "in" the market, or "holding a position overnight." The risks give them their "high." When they aren't trading, they experience extreme tension. To ease this tension, they start trading, and relief comes regardless of the success of the trade. The results of their actions are secondary; they just need to trade. Typically, addicted traders must be trading all the time to find relief from the problems and bad feelings in their lives. Profit and loss become secondary. Trading is all that matters. Of course, when you lose sight of the goal—winning—the losses start to mount.

Case Study

Peter C., An Addicted Trader

Peter C., single and 30 years old, worked through the Board of Trade in the time-honored manner. He started as a runner on the floor and eventually wound up a phone man, placing orders for a large agricultural company in the soybean pit. He learned how the soybean pit operated, how and when the market moved. He saw who made money and who lost it. He felt he could do better, but he didn't have enough money to buy a seat on the exchange. He decided to leave the floor and took a job "upstairs" as a broker/trader in a local brokerage house. This gave him the opportunity to earn more money, as well as to trade for his own account.

Peter had always been a gregarious, outgoing person. He had done fairly well in high school. He had been popular and active, starring in a few of the major drama productions, such as *Macbeth* and *West Side Story*. Everyone always thought that he had a flair for the dramatic.

Peter had a lot of friends who were very loyal to him. He was always well liked for his carefree style and admired for his ability to "let go" and take risks. He had a penchant for doing unconventional things, such as skinny-dipping in the lake or confronting his high-school principal about the dress code.

Because of his nonconformity, Peter's friends were surprised when he took a job as a runner at the Board. They assumed it would be too boring and run-of-the-mill for Peter. But he was excited by the billions of dollars that passed through the Exchange every day. To him, it was the center of the universe, and he had every intention of claiming a portion of those passing billions for himself one day.

Believing that a system was necessary to do well, Peter learned to use a "volume/momentum" computer trading program from one of his fellow traders and began to trade the grains markets, since he had observed these markets as a runner and felt familiar with them. But he found that this system didn't always seem to work for him. His initial problem was that his system rarely gave him an entry signal.

After two weeks, Peter became bored with trading soybeans, although he was sure he could outdo the locals in that pit. He was anxious to utilize the huge leverage that his brokerage position offered. It was time to "get on with it." He decided to trade gold. He felt gold was classier; it sounded good, and so he was sure he would do well.

After three days in the gold market, Peter still had not received an entry signal, so he abandoned the volume/momentum system. He figured he would wing it for a while and try his luck without a system, but he would never tell anyone for fear that they would think him crazy. He bought two contracts and waited. After he'd made about $300, he sold them both. He was quite satisfied with the trades, but felt he should try another system.

Peter invested his profits in a system that used moving averages, stochastics, and volume "surges." However, using this system, he still didn't get any entry signals. He bought two more contracts on "instinct," but this time the market moved against him. His system quickly gave him a sell signal, so he sold his contracts, but didn't go short. He lost $1000.

Peter was unconcerned. He told his boss that he'd have the balance owed to the firm within three days, which was customary. He immediately sold two contracts short, but the market stabilized. He borrowed the money from a friend and held his position. The gold market did nothing for about two weeks. Peter started to feel tense and fidgety. He knew he could pay off his friend—he'd already given him $150 of it—that wasn't the problem. It was the waiting that was driving him crazy. He looked back at the soybean market and saw that it was breaking down. He sold two soybean contracts short and made another $300 within a few days. He was beginning to feel that he was getting the hang of trading, and he had reduced his debt to only $500.

In the meantime, Peter made no phone calls and brought in no new business to the firm. His boss told him to come in during the evening to make some "cold calls," but Peter had forgotten. Eventually, he was told that if he didn't show more enthusiasm and responsibility, he would have to find work elsewhere. Peter looked more intensely at the gold and soybean markets but nothing was happening. The waiting made him extremely anxious, even more so than before.

Peter became tempted by the currency markets and sold two contracts of the Japanese yen short. He lost $2500 when the market moved swiftly against him due to the lowering of the U.S. short-term interest rates. Two days later, Peter was asked to leave the firm, not because of the margin he owed, but rather because he had done such an inadequate job of serving customers.

Peter intended to pay back the money he owed to the firm once he found a new position as a trader. He felt he really needed much more capital to demonstrate his true trading potential. He thought about trying to get some customers to allow him to trade for them. Above all else, he wanted to get back in the game and knew he'd find a way to do it.

Dependence and Tolerance

Peter is an example of the addicted investor. He is no longer in control of his need to trade. He also displays two key characteristics of his addiction—tolerance and dependence.

Dependence means that the individual has become "hooked." Either the body or the mind "needs" to gamble. Thus, either physiological or psychological forces are at work beyond your control. You are powerless to stop them. In fact, without them, you become anxious and tense—symptoms of a "withdrawal" of sorts. Remember Peter's anxiety when he was forced to stop trading for even a few days?

To gauge your level of possible addiction, answer the following questions. Place a mark next to those questions that you respond to with "yes":

When you stop investing or trading for a while (assuming you have no open positions), do you:

1. Become apprehensive and fidgety—pace a lot?

2. Worry about the markets excessively or compulsively?

3. Experience feelings of being out of control?

When you are actively trading, do you:

4. Often trade more than you intend to?

5. Feel guilty about the amount of trading/investing you are involved with?

6. Continue to trade although it is adversely affecting your life?

7. Spend excessive amounts of time in activities related to the market?

8. Try unsuccessfully to limit the amount of time, money, or energy you put into investing?

9. Forgo important social, occupational, or recreational activities because you are fearful and anxious about being away from the markets?

If you answered "yes" to three or more of the above, you may have a psychological dependence on investing or trading.

Tolerance is the second hallmark of addiction. If you have raised your tolerance, it will take larger and larger amounts of the substance—in this case, your investments or trades—to produce the same physical and psychological effects. In our example, Peter had to move up from grains to gold and yen to satisfy his growing tolerance for trading.

The good news for the addicted investor is that addictions can be controlled. If you're aware you're addicted, you can monitor the effect it's having not only on your trades, but on your life. The worst thing you can do is fool yourself—to insist that you can "stop any time I want" or that "it's really not a big problem." That's when you lose your shirt. We've taken five "life" areas and divided them into stages of addiction. Determine which stage describes your addiction in each of the following areas:

1. *Social.* At first, most members of your social circle are old friends or relatives. As you become more compulsive, you find that you spend less time with these friends, and more time with fellow traders and investors. Finally, you find that you associate only with "hard-core" traders and investors and that your free time is spent discussing the market, and little else.

2. *Work.* At first, your performance at work is steady and relatively normal. Then you begin having problems with absenteeism, and you often come in late, which affects your performance. Finally, your job is in

jeopardy because you're preoccupied with trading and investing; you may even become tempted to steal or embezzle money for trading.

3. *Personal Hygiene.* In the beginning, your sleep, appetite, and grooming remain normal, but soon you no longer eat right and are losing sleep. Finally, you may begin to suffer from chronic sleep deprivation, your appearance suffers, and you may experience frequent physical mishaps and accidents.

4. *Money.* At first, you don't lose a significant amount, and you remain untroubled by your losses. Then you overspend and may find yourself forced to borrow money or use a lot of leverage, asking for frequent financial favors. Finally, you run headlong into financial ruin.

5. *Emotions.* At first, you "gamble" in the markets because you enjoy it, or are curious. Next, you trade to fend off feelings of depression or guilt. You begin to suffer from mood swings. Finally, you trade or invest to feel "normal." You are totally preoccupied and can't seem to stop, even if you wanted to.

ACTION PLAN FOR THE ADDICTED INVESTOR

If you're in the early or middle stages of addiction, your awareness of your problem may go a long way toward solving it. By recognizing your addictive tendencies and how they can hamper your investing success, you can keep a wary eye on your behavior for the telltale signs discussed here.

If you're in later stages of addiction, however, you should seek psychological counseling. It's highly unlikely that you'll be able to quit cold turkey. Without someone to help you get at the psychological source of your addiction, you'll return to it sooner or later.

Without that help, you could be in a lot of trouble. The following is a cautionary tale for addicted investors who deny their problem.

Case Study

Michael P., Hooked on Losing

Michael P. was an up-and-coming commodities CTA (certified trading advisor) who had been trading for about three years. He seemed to have a knack for it and quickly developed a following. Michael traded T-bonds, stock index futures, and gold and silver futures. He had a small office in Manhattan and many of his old friends from New York University referred clients to him.

At the relatively young age of 28, Michael thought that things were going pretty well for him. He seemed to have caught the wave of the bull market in the mid-1980s, and a large brokerage house was thinking of backing him as a major money manager. He took risks, but things usually worked out for him. He traded for his own account and had done very well for himself.

After the 1987 crash, most CTAs cut back on the amount of leverage and risk they took on, but Michael felt that 1987 was simply a minor setback for him. He had not been hurt badly by the crash, although several of his accounts had dropped out, while the remainder had set limits on what they were willing to risk.

At about this time, Michael's friends began to notice changes in his behavior. They claimed he was always talking about the marketplace. He had stopped dating altogether so that he could focus all his energies on the markets. He even stopped going to the theater, which he had enjoyed a great deal. It seemed that as more of his clients pulled out, he felt a more urgent need to trade. He often indulged that need, sometimes engaging in risky trades or even trading against the wishes of his clients. Finally, one of his clients threatened to sue him after discovering he had traded stock-index futures in the account after the client had expressly forbidden it in writing.

Although Michael's' performance was not disastrous, he was losing. This only led to his desire to trade with more frequency. He then lost on some very large, risky T-bond trades, and 75 percent of his accounts closed out. He was named in three civil lawsuits for misappropriation of funds. Michael was careening out of control.

As Michael's desperation grew, so did the scope of his addiction. Eventually, Michael began using cocaine. He felt that if he had more energy, he would be able to win back what he had lost. By this time, Michael was trading for his own account and had lost three quarters of his assets.

It got worse. In late 1989, based on a tip from one of his former clients, Michael was arrested after the New York Police Department searched his office and seized a gram of cocaine. His career was now over. Because of the lawsuits, he was forced into Chapter 7 and lost the little that he had left. Michael had hit bottom.

It took two years for him to recover. Michael joined both Gamblers Anonymous and Narcotics Anonymous. He came to understand that he had an "addictive" personality. He began attending weekly group therapy, which he found to be insight producing and supportive. Eventually, Michael got a job as a broker at a commodities firm in Manhattan on a probationary basis. However, Michael didn't trade for himself or his clients, and he stayed off drugs. After a year, that probation was lifted. Like any addict, Michael isn't and will never be cured. To think otherwise would be an open invitation for the events of previous years to repeat themselves.

THE SOCIOPATHIC TRADER (AKA THE CON MAN)

Whether it's a broker, a money manager, a fellow investor, or a cold caller promising you millions, at some point you will run into a hard-core sociopath. These people are often skilled, smooth, articulate, and persuasive. They can strip you of your assets, encourage you to take on liabilities you never thought you'd take on, and have you thank them for it. It doesn't matter how intelligent, perceptive, or experienced you are. It can happen to anyone.

Although most brokers and traders are legitimate, there are those who do not have your best interests in mind. Ordinary con artists are fairly easy to spot; you feel as if you should wash your hands after shaking theirs. But sociopaths are patient as well as clever. The "setup" can take a long time. They may seem legitimate. They can place orders for you in the usual fashion or enjoy a favorable reputation. Their references will be good.

However, sooner or later, you will be "invited" to join an "elite" group that they trade for. The opportunity may even be understated, yet the implication is not. The message is "If you use me for your investments, then you will be on the inside track and your profits will grow astronomically." In most instances, the real risks involved when joining this group are never explicitly laid out for you. You are lured into taking chances you would never ordinarily take, all because you have unknowingly decided to trust a sociopath.

Let's take a look at a typical investment scam. Though this particular scenario involves real estate rather than the financial markets, the modus operandi is the same.

Case Study

Albert U., Real Estate Shark

Al was a real estate broker who was known to be on the "fast track." He worked out of expensive offices in Los Angeles and supposedly had quite a wealthy and worldly client base.

Al would routinely examine his firm's client list, noting who had recently sold or purchased a new home. He would then check in with them about the value of their home and their future real estate plans. During the course of this conversation, the client would inevitably ask for Al's opinion on the current state of the market. Al would respond that certain parts of the market were pure dynamite, that business was going quite well, and that they should let him know if they were ever interested in investing. When asked about what he was involved with now, Al would mention a few parts of West Los Angeles that everyone knew were "up and coming." He would further note that he had no partnership units available at that time, but that he might in the future.

A few months later, Al would call again to chat, asking general questions about their real estate to make it seem like a genuine customer service call. Frequently, the client would recall the previous conversation and inquire again about the general market conditions. Al would comment that the market was stable in general, but that there was a lot of activity in certain areas. Then Al would comment that he was in the process of putting something together.

About a month later, a packet of information would arrive at the client's home that provided details of a modest investment. Al always tried to make the first deal small and successful. And he never took big fees out of that first deal.

The first investment any client made would be moderately successful and return a small profit. It was meant to give the client a false sense of security, creating a desire for more. The second and third investments were usually much larger and involved a great deal more risk in terms of personal guarantees to banks. Al worked with an accountant and convinced many of his clients that it was much easier to use him as their own accountant, since real estate investments were generally tied into tax deductions.

Al began buying and reselling large commercial buildings in Los Angeles—a very risky market. After three or four residential deals, however, his clients were used to working with him and had confidence in him. Unfortunately, that confidence was costing them more and more with each new deal.

After the first deal, Al's firm would typically take a large fee for putting the partnership together. He would also take a large fee for "brokering" the property, a large fee for managing the property, and a large fee for selling the property. On top of that, Al would receive a generous referral fee from the accountant for each new client he brought in. As long as his clients were making money, they never challenged Al on his fees, although some thought the charges were outrageous.

Al would periodically mention that it was getting more and more difficult to include his longstanding clients in new deals when so many others were itching to get in on new projects. He even claimed to have discussed major ventures with movie stars eager to invest. The message he was sending was clear: "You can be easily replaced by someone a lot more attractive than you." Al was a master sociopath.

Al began to insist that his clients sign over power of attorney to him, originally for the "sake of the closing" on the properties. He would rarely forward documents to longtime clients, even though they were involved in several major deals. He would wrongly use the power of attorney in other ways as well, making sure that his clients were personally liable to the banks and other creditors.

On a client's first small deal, Al would always put up an insignificant amount of his own money, and he made sure the client knew that he had invested funds in the property. When Al suggested bigger deals at a later date, he would remind the clients that he was always in on them too, risking his own money. While this made the client feel more confident about the risk, it was a lie. Al transferred all the liability to his "marks."

Al began to buy progressively larger commercial pieces. If one started to collapse, he would shift money around as long as possible to keep the house of cards from tumbling down around him. Few of his clients had access to the books, so no one really knew what he was doing. And, at each stage of the game, Al would still collect high fees, while sharing none of the liability and responsibility.

When a few buildings went into default, Al cashed out and left for Mexico. He had become quite wealthy and hired two full-time lawyers just to handle the lawsuits that were subsequently filed, making sure that he never had to declare bankruptcy. He closed down his real estate operation and left his accountant to face some very angry clients. Up to the very end, Al tried to get new clients into new deals so that he might keep his operation going just a little bit longer before making a hasty exit. In fact, the majority of his clients had no idea that the projects had gone into default until they received notices from the bank. They had never thought to check to make sure that the money Al obtained by signing for them with a power of attorney was being used to pay off the banks.

Profile of a Sociopath

Most sociopathic con artists are very careful to cover their tracks and appear to be above board. But there are some clues you can look for when appraising someone's character and potential.

Modern psychiatry defines someone as having an "antisocial" personality if he or she has had significant troubles before the age of 15, combined with current patterns of irresponsible and antisocial behavior.

The traits in the following list are common to sociopaths. The sociopath may be smart enough to hide these traits from you, especially if he or she is a broker soliciting your business. Still, if you learn that a broker or advisor possesses some of these traits, we advise extreme caution:

- Poor work history
- Frequent unexplained absences
- Impulsive and frequent quitting of jobs
- Long periods of unemployment
- Habitual harassment of others
- Stealing
- Pursuing an illegal occupation (drug-dealing, gambling, fraud, etc.)

- Child abuse
- Repeated fighting
- Defaulting on debts
- Failure to pay child support
- Frequent moving of residence
- Lying
- Recklessness with regard to safety (drunk driving, speeding)
- Irresponsible parenting
- Repeated squandering of money on frivolous items
- Self-centeredness
- Promiscuity
- Lack of remorse

You may have noticed a reassuring theme in these traits: They describe someone who lacks a conscience.

No Regrets

A person who displays these traits is not simply a "selfish" person. Take Al. Al didn't really care about anyone but himself, but more than that, he didn't care if someone else got hurt or suffered from his actions. This is an example of the true sociopath. It didn't matter how much money was lost by someone else who put their trust in him. It could be a little, it could be a lot. To Al, it was simply "not my problem." Al felt no remorse. While Al displayed some of the traits in the preceding list (fraudulent behavior, failure to honor financial obligations, frequent moving from place to place), the main reason we would classify him as a sociopath is his total lack of conscience—his lack of remorse.

Can you get hurt by this type of investor or trader? Yes! It is important that you be careful about the contracts you enter into with money managers, CTAs and brokers of any kind. Although there are very few such individuals around, it only takes one to devastate scores of investors. It sometimes pays to be cautious. If you have any hesitations or doubts about your broker or advisor, take the time to research his or her background, or gather information on the deals he or she offers. Make sure you see all the contracts all the time. Always insist on documentation. Check references that are "out of the loop." Ask for the names of other investors, and make sure the firm itself is reputable and stable. And make sure you confront your broker with any and all inconsistencies. If you still have doubts, get out of the relationship. Pay attention to your suspicions—a little bit of "fussiness" might be beneficial in this case.

Why is the con so effective? Perhaps the most amazing thing about sociopaths is their ability to tune into their clients. They have an uncanny sense of empathy and seem easily to put themselves in your shoes. They make you feel understood.

Empathy can make you do just about anything. You hire a psychotherapist to understand you—but you hire a broker or CTA to make money for you. Psychiatrists know that "feeling understood" can have a most powerful influence on a person. Deep in our hearts, there is an overwhelming need to feel understood. Thus, to possess empathy is to possess a valuable commodity indeed. The white-collar sociopath is a master of empathy, which he uses for harmful purposes.

CHAPTER 16

Ten Rules for Smart Trading

Up to this point, we've looked at investing/trading from an inside-out perspective. Our focus has been on how the inner mental marketplace affects your trading in the financial one. From previous chapters, you should know the psychological investing type that is pertinent to you, and how to invest most successfully given your own particular profile.

But what happens when you're involved in an actual trade; when you're caught up in the process of making a critical investment decision? To complement the insight you now possess, we think it's important that you be armed with some psychologically sound trading rules that cut across the investor types and that give you guidelines when you're faced with typical trading scenarios and the decisions they demand.

Keep the following 10 rules in mind as you journey from your inner to outer marketplace.

Rule 1: Don't pick tops or bottoms when position trading. Let the markets tell you when trends turn.

Too much good money is thrown away anticipating, rather than following, trend changes.

This rule is easy to follow if you're the ideal psychological type—self-actualized, self-aware, self-satisfied, acutely attuned to your inner investing-self.

Unfortunately, very few of us are in such an ideal category. As a result, we break this rule with impunity. If you are a masked investor, for instance, you don your mask of greatness and decide you can do no wrong; you gamble that your prediction of where the market is heading will be accurate. To fulfill your self-image of a great investor, a master of the universe (to borrow Tom Wolfe's phrase), you have to win big. In reality, you aren't investing to win big; you're investing to validate your self-image.

You may also break this rule because you're ambivalent and conflicted. One day you're an investor who's out to make a killing, the next you're someone who just wants to make an acceptable profit. It all goes back to ambiguous attitudes toward money, and you can no more control those attitude swings than you can changes in the weather.

For instance, you decide that you want to go with the trend and position trade. You notice that silver has risen 5 percent in price with large volume over the past few days, on the heels of a long period of consolidation. So you move in. But you're continually trying to figure out where the top will be. Then you change your mind about following the trend and get out.

Your decisions are based on an internal conflict between striking it rich and making a reasonable profit. As a result, your investing strategy is contradictory. One day, you're taking big risks trying to predict trends; the next day you're avoiding risk and deciding that you can't possibly know where the market is heading.

If you're a masked investor or if you are facing an internal conflict (especially as it relates to money), follow this rule at all costs.

Rule 2: Don't hang on to losing positions thinking they will turn around. Learning how to take small losses is important.

Investors frequently confront this scenario: They're losing money, but they find themselves unable to cut their losses and run. Instead of a small loss, they end up with a big one.

Why? If you're like most investors, you'd probably respond, "I was sure it was going to turn around." Why were you sure? Was your assumption based on solid evidence? Or was there something inside you that refused to let go of the loser?

If the latter was the case, and if you want to learn how to let go the next time, consider the following three problems:

1. *Getting Even.* Revenging investors, beware of this desire! You have difficulty accepting a loss. To you, it's a rejection by the market, and you can't stand rejection. Therefore, you try to get even. How? By hanging on to a losing investment in the vain hope that it will somehow reward you for your loyalty. Sure, it could happen. The woman you loved and lost three years ago might also have a change of heart and come back to you. But it's unlikely. Don't try and get even. Get out while the getting is good—or at least not overly bad.

2. *Machismo.* Or should we say, masochism? Deep down, you hold on to a losing position to prove you're not a coward; you're not going to be the one to run when things get tough. It hurts to lose, but you can take it. So, you put on the mask of the brave, heroic captain on the ship. You may even become self-righteous in defense of your investment, claiming that while the others are abandoning ship, you'll remain at the helm. Such a stance might "feel" good—at least until the ship goes down. Don't torture yourself with losers. Get out in time and with sufficient financial reserves to fight another day.

3. *Fear of Success.* Here, you are like Oedipus on Wall Street. You hold on to a losing position because deep down inside, you don't want to win. Sound ridiculous? Then why keep a loser when every advisor and statistic tells you to get rid of it? Because of events that took place early in your life—often an intensely competitive relationship with a same-sex parent—you're afraid of doing well. It's one of the reasons why great athletes throw away their careers on drugs and alcohol; it's why very talented people end up squandering their talent. Success is scary. So against all rhyme or reason, you stack the deck against yourself. These conflicts are deep. This is a serious problem, and it often requires serious therapy to escape the trap.

Listen to this internal dialogue of an investor, and see if it sounds familiar:

I'm going for it! I deserve success just as much as anyone else. Oh boy, if that OEX moves upward. I'm in! My timing is perfect. Wait a second, it's turning. It's going the other way. Is this serious or is this temporary? Still going the other way, and I'm losing money. When is this going to turn around? This is going to cost me a bundle. I better get out. But maybe if I wait, it's bound to turn around, right? I can't believe this is happening. Going down further. Okay. Just stick with it. Get out now and I'm a loser. Just give it a little time and things are going to get better, they have to.

Though the dialogue would normally take place over a much longer period of time than this condensed version, it makes the point. Notice all the rationalizations that keep this investor hooked to a losing proposition. He's obviously conflicted—he knows he should get out, but he can't translate that knowledge into action.

Rule 3: Put in stop-loss orders to help avoid being at the mercy of markets that move against you.

Why wouldn't someone follow this logical advice?

A lot of reasons. First, there's denial: "I just don't want to think about what's wrong with this trade/investment." You refuse even to consider the possibility that your trade might go awry, that the market might move against you. Unbridled optimism might be fine in certain situations, but given the harsh realities of the investment world, it's an unrealistic attitude. Masked investors frequently resort to this denial; their masks of invulnerability don't allow the possibility of defeat.

Revenging investors, too, often fall into this trap. They've already loved and lost. Putting a stop in would force them to think about that loss; and it hurts too much to think about that. By avoiding the issue of stops, they avoid the issue of loss, until they are swamped by it.

Some investors substitute "mental" stops for real ones. They tell themselves: "I won't put a stop in, but in my mind I'll know when to stop the losses." This mental stop gives investors greater freedom of choice; they're not locked into a predetermined exit point that could toss them out of the game. The only problem with this strategy, of course, is when they fail to act on their mental stop; they play with a new mental stop point, and more losses occur.

Finally, paranoid investors avoid stops because they can't stand the thought of any more losses. They're people with financial suicide in mind; every trade is a jump off a steep cliff, and they don't want to survey the rocks below. A stop would force them to survey the damage a loss would bring. Without one, they can jump blind and hope against hope that they'll land on a soft, winning trade.

Rule 4: Know when to hold 'em, not just when to fold 'em.

Some investors are very good at cutting their losses, but they're not so good when it comes to holding a position or increasing it. It all comes down to being "psychologically able" to win.

As strange as it may seem, not everyone is. Depressed investors, for example, are frequently threatened by success. Their underlying image is one of worthlessness, and they can't conceive that they are right about a winning stock or of one of their trades being on the mark.

Put it in another context. You've all heard about people who won the lottery and had enormous difficulty adjusting to their newfound riches: They squandered the money on ridiculous things, were tremendously unhappy, lost their friends, went through a divorce.

Granted, there's a difference between a lottery winner and an investor. But the principle behind adjusting to winning is the same: Success is difficult to handle. In anticipation of that success, some investors unconsciously pull back from winning positions prematurely, refusing to deal with the success those positions bring.

Have you even taken profits too soon? Think about why. Did you really think it was the right time? Or was it something else?

Some people feel uncomfortable with the envy that comes with success; they want to be one of the guys, not a top dog that everyone is trying to cut down to size. Or it could be that you don't want to be seen as greedy—one of those distasteful creatures who lust after money for its own sake.

These fears have prompted more than one investor to jump ship on profitable positions. Perhaps you're a victim of that Wall Street adage, "Bulls make money, bears make money, and pigs get slaughtered." Like all adages, there's a grain of truth in it. But masked investors (to single out one type) take it as gospel. Vitally concerned about their internal images, masked investors are content to take small, safe profits and maintain their nice guy personas.

That sanctimonious voice you hear whispering in your ear is called your conscience, and it can turn you into a financial wimp. It insists, "Money makes you a bad person"; "Money is the root of all evil"; "Money corrupts." If you're a depressed investor or a conflicted one, the volume of that voice rises a few decibels: "You're selfish"; "You're only interested in your self."

Don't believe that voice. If you're like most people, you do not resemble the Gordon Gecko character in the movie *Wall Street,* who proclaims, "Greed is Good." Instead, you're simply someone looking to make money to better your own life or that of your family. You're not hurting anyone else by profiting from your investing. In fact, you can tell that nattering little voice that your investing is helping the economy as well as the people you invest with and the companies you invest in.

To adhere to Rule 4, analyze your motivations before pulling back from a winner. If you see market forces or receive other information indicating that the winner will soon be a loser, fine, get rid of it. But if your impulse is dictated by some vague feeling of unease or a nameless fear, be skeptical. Winners are tough to find, so once you've latched on to this precious commodity, don't give it up without a solid reason.

Rule 5: Don't add on to a losing trade (unless there are unusual circumstances). When buying, each new purchase should be higher, and when selling, each new sale should be lower.

Contrary to common sense, we break this rule all the time, especially after losses. Who hasn't been gulled by the carnival barker's cry, "Double or nothing," after losing at a rigged game.

For the revenging investor, the motivation to get even is just too much. You're going to respond to the market's challenge. The problem: It's tough to accept a loss. It's the coward's way out. Better to hang in there—better for your self-image. Unfortunately, it's worse for your pocketbook.

Why is it so hard to buy at a higher price? After all, the investor asks, "If I was right and bought low and can sell high, why would I want to buy high?" Because you were right. If you are buying higher than you originally did, you are buying with the trend. That's hard for many investors to accept. Many investors we've surveyed and worked with have great difficulty believing that they're "good enough" to win.

Why is it hard to add on to a successful trade at a higher price? The paranoid investor might worry, "If I add on at a higher price, I may lose what I've already gained." Such investors are questioning their self-worth; they don't trust their decision-making capacity. They sentence themselves to investing limbo, that middle ground between success and failure.

Rule 6: Never place stops just above daily highs or just below daily lows. Floor traders frequently run stops and these levels are often violated.

If you happen to be a fussy investor, obsessing over all the details, you're likely to break this rule. You get so caught up in trading formulas that the flexibility this rule demands scares you. Tight stops give you a sense of order, which you desperately need. As odd as it seems, you'd rather lose money than be "messy" in your trading.

Cautious paranoid investors are also likely to ignore this rule. Whenever there is a known trading range—for a work of art as well as a stock index future—cautious investors are at risk. The uncertainty that lurks at the corners of the range does them in. Not knowing who to trust, these investors resort to formulas: They provide an illusory shield against the market's potential to hurt them.

If you know yourself to be a cautious or fussy investor, integrate flexibility into your trading strategy.

Without it, you could lock yourself into a formula for financial failure.

> **Rule 7: When in a winning day trade position, get out "market on close." Day traders are usually unwilling to take positions overnight, so they will exit their trades, adding fuel to a market's direction on close.**

One would think that if a trader changed a game plan in midstream from day trading to position trading and because of that, took a beating, that one big loss would make him forsake that strategy.

But I'm sure you know people who change investing strategies in midstream all the time. They start with a sound investing strategy. Yet they depart from it at the drop of a hat—or even the slightest drop in the market.

People who are most susceptible to "fickle" investing are depressed investors; their low self-esteem is the culprit. When someone—a broker, a friend—advises, "Now that you have a winner, let your profits run, keep it going," you automatically move from day trading to position trading. You're extraordinarily vulnerable to the advice of others. You may switch gears the next day when the newspaper reports an event that seems to dictate a new tack.

There's a key psychological variable behind getting out of your winning day trade at market-on-close. To do so, you not only have to know how the external game is played, but be attuned to the motivations of others. Put yourself in the shoes of other committed day traders who refuse to carry a trade overnight. If you're long during the day and are winning, the traders on the other side are losing. They may wait until the very end to get out, but they'll get out because they're committed to the day only.

On the other hand, day traders who sold must buy back to even out their trades. If they do that at the end of the day (especially at the last possible moment), then the market may accelerate even more in your direction.

If you close out your own winning day trade too far in advance of the close, then you may lose this extra benefit.

Though this is similar to our earlier rule of not bailing out of a winning trade too soon, there's an "extra credit" element here. It's not enough to know your internal market; you should know what's motivating it. The correct term is empathy. You're not going to be able to develop it overnight. It usually comes after you become accustomed to winning. You can then reach out toward others and probe their trading motivations. What are they worried about? What are they likely to do under various trading circumstances?

Rule 8: When day trading, look for the lunch hour bubble. Markets which trend in the morning, quiet down around 12:00 NOON (CST) when traders and fund managers go to lunch.

The real rule here is: Seize the golden opportunities.

If you don't trust yourself, if you're suspicious of your instincts, you'll miss opportunities such as the lunch hour bubble. Your senses will relay the information, you'll process it, but you won't be able to act on it. You'll start second-guessing yourself, irrationally questioning what you've observed.

Depressed investors often are insecure; they also react slowly. The best investors spot exit and entry points with uncanny precision: They know instinctively when to get in and out of a trade, and they don't hesitate. Perhaps they make some mistakes. But they refuse to let good trades pass them by. They grab enough of them to come out ahead.

It's not enough to "see" an opportunity; you have to seize it. Our revenging investor will probably be able to do this; our conflicted investor probably won't. People in this latter category will react to an opportunity with, "What if I win? What if I lose?" They're like shoppers who see an undeniably great deal in a store but can't take the final step and make the purchase. They wonder, "Do I really need this item? If I keep shopping, I might find an even better product. My wife is going to be mad at me for even spending money on something like this."

All the conflicting questions roll around in your head, and you're paralyzed. You just can't break through the puzzle to act. And as you know, the markets wait for no one.

A fussy investor may also run into trouble when opportunity knocks. Mr. Fussy may have an overly compulsive or rigid approach to entering or exiting markets. Though that approach might be sound, it isn't foolproof. The markets are messy; they can be chaotic, surprising, and contrary. To refuse to seize opportunities because they are unexpected or don't fit into your system is a possible danger for fussy investors. Similarly, fussy investors can spot opportunities easily enough, but they may be unable to act on them quickly; they must check and recheck their system before making a move, and by then it is too late.

There is one additional lesson to be learned from the lunch hour bubble rule, and it's applicable to all psychological trading types. The bubble provides you with a second chance at a move, a moment of freedom where you can get in or out of a trade.

Think about how often you seize that opportunity. Do you give yourself a second chance to correct a bad investing move? We've found that many investors are so hard on themselves, they refuse to take this opportunity to make a correction. They spend so much psychological time chiding themselves for their stupidity that opportunities to be smart slip right past them.

Rule 9: Don't take a "flyer" in front of a large market report. It's more than likely you won't predict the exact outcome, and the markets may have already discounted the report prior to its release.

Taking a flyer in front of a large market report is similar to rolling down Niagara Falls in a barrel. It will either be the most incredible ride of your life or you'll be smashed to bits on the rocks below. Which do you think is more likely to occur? Clearly, the risk outweighs the reward. Yet, people take the risk and the reason is addiction.

Most investors understand how addictive investing can be. It's a rush, a kick of adrenaline. Some of us are addicted to high risk. Over time, we develop an unhealthy tolerance for it and dependence on it. It skews our investing perspective until risk/reward rations become meaningless.

Sometimes, addicted investors are like alcoholics; they don't know when they're addicted. They rationalize, "I'm just a social drinker—I can stop when I want."

Do you take crazy risks? Examine the following three psychological types and see if your risk taking fits in one of them.

Masked investors put on a tough guy disguise and shout, "Look at me! I'm so smart and confident that I can predict the future and stand out there and battle the market forces." Sometimes masked investors will guess right and win. This only serves to reinforce their grandiose self-vision. They'll continue to up the ante until they're wiped out in one fatal trade—that's all it takes.

Unlike masked investors, those who are depressed slog along with a low-risk strategy until they become desperate. In a futile, last-gasp attempt to salvage their low self-esteem and decaying self-image, they'll do something totally out of character—place a huge amount of money on a stock they've never invested in before, for instance. Unless they're incredibly lucky, the investment won't pay off. How can it? They are taking an irrational risk based on their psychological type, not on any well-planned strategy.

Fussy investors, too, don't make a habit of high-risk investing. Because they are orderly and circumspect, taking a flyer is generally out of character. Yet, at some point, they may take that flyer in the vain hope that a big win will provide them with the control they want. Though fussy investors are the least likely of the three types discussed here to take a flyer, some critical life event (a messy divorce, an increasingly chaotic job) may prompt them to take leave of their senses and go for broke.

Rule 10: Don't trade thin markets. Markets with poor open interest (or few outstanding shares) and little daily volume present problems because of the wide discrepancy in bid and ask prices.

It's difficult if not impossible to make much money in thin markets. It's like playing penny-ante poker: There's not much point to a game if the stakes are absurdly low.

But some investors are attracted to these markets. One reason: they're afraid of getting hurt or hurting others, of winning or losing. For an anxious, conflicted investor, thin markets are a place to rest, where nothing much happens, good or bad. You can drift there forever. Of course, what is the point?

For depressed investors, thin markets are attractive because they require relatively little energy, enthusiasm, and concentration. Depressed investors lack all these qualities—they have to struggle to get out of bed in the morning. Since there's little liquidity to move these markets, they allow depressed investors to drift in the trading doldrums.

Finally, there are all the loners and the cautious and paranoid investors who seek safe havens in thin markets. Protection and isolation attract them. They're looking for the desert islands of investing. If no one else is there, nobody will stick a knife in their backs.

Either you're an investor or trader, or you're not. Better not to trade at all than to be in thin markets.

CHAPTER 17

Keeping the Right Distance Between Your Mind and Your Money

Money flows in and out of your mind just as it flows in and out of your pocket. What's your attitude toward that flow? What does it mean to you? By now you should know that the meaning of money extends beyond your bank account or what you can buy with it. Money is loaded with meaning, depending on who you are and the circumstances you're in.

We have discussed how money has different meanings for different types of investors. Let's spend a moment reviewing how each investor type defines money in order to understand how a person might be more concerned about money flowing into the mind rather than the bank account.

1. *The* Masked *Investor.* "Money will make others proud of me and make me proud, too."

2. *The* Depressed *Investor.* "Money will make me happy."

3. *The* Revenging *Investor.* "With money, I can beat those who have beaten me."

4. *The* Fussy *Investor.* "Money keeps me together—without it, I'd fall apart."

5. *The* Paranoid *Investor.* "Having money means I can't get hurt."

6. *The* Conflicted *Investor.* "Money will make me a winner, but what will I lose?"

Each type differs according to the flow, or "motion" of money in the mind—how it occupies, consoles, encourages, and simply keeps the investor from feeling uncertain and afraid.

And yet, money can flow out of our minds as well: At certain time, money will be the last thing on our minds. There may be times when our emotional or psychological needs are fulfilled, or times when our financial situation seems so hopeless that to forget and ignore it, if only for a short while, is our best defense.

Wise and successful investors are able to control and maintain the psychological distance between themselves and their money; they have learned when to concentrate on money (getting close), and when it is beneficial to forget about it and focus on the other aspects of life (pushing it away).

Case Study

Alice W., Conflicted Number-Cruncher

Alice was a Phi Beta Kappa and summa cum laude graduate of Vassar. She went into finance because she loved playing with and manipulating numbers. Both her parents had been teachers at private prep schools, and although they were not wealthy, Alice and her siblings were able to live on beautiful campuses while attending those schools for free. In addition, her parents' positions gave Alice an opportunity to befriend the children of many prominent families—children who were destined one day to run many of America's largest corporations.

Although much of Alice's childhood was filled with beauty and education, her home life was less than happy. Her parents constantly fought about money. While they were always stressing that "money isn't everything," it seemed to be a source of daily friction. Her father insisted that they cut corners where they could; they seldom ate out and her mother sewed clothes instead of buying them in the expensive department stores. Even as a child, Alice was determined to live life differently when she was an adult.

As she grew, Alice became conflicted. She was torn between a career in which she would use her intellectual powers and a career in which she might be able to make a lot of money. Her parents had loved math and had always encouraged her to learn; after college graduation, Alice had taught math for one year at a prep school.

Although she enjoyed it, she decided to put her love of numbers to a more practical and profitable use. She joined one of the country's largest brokerage firms and worked hard for three years. By calling the old contacts she had made in school, she successfully developed a broad client base, specializing in the bond market.

Alice met and married a brilliant mathematician from Columbia University. Through him, she was able to keep up with the world of academic mathematics. Her husband made a small but respectable salary, but they depended on Alice's steadily increasing income. Eventually, they had two children. Although Alice continued to work full time, which provided the family with more than sufficient income, she occasionally felt obligated to sew some of her daughter's dresses herself.

Throughout her career, Alice had been presented with opportunities to advance, but had refused each offer. Soon after she married, Alice had been offered a position as a bond trader. Alice had thought that she could do well at it, and the firm had assured her that she could have her old job back if she was unhappy trading, but she had turned it down anyway, although she wasn't quite sure why.

A few years later, Alice had been asked to become a junior economist. Her firm had even offered to send her to night school so that she could earn her PhD. It was a very attractive offer, and her husband had pledged to support her decision. Although it would have required a small cut in pay, Alice would have been able to exercise her love for numbers, use her analytical skills, and become more involved in the world of academia—all of which she had desired. And in the long run, Alice would have had the opportunity to obtain an even larger salary, with the possibility of earning additional money for conducting lectures and workshops.

But Alice declined the offer, fearing that the change would have brought too much stress to the family, financially and otherwise. Because of her fears, she had cut short the path for advancement and was now feeling very unsatisfied professionally.

Alice began psychotherapy to help her understand her decision. She began doing all the right things, such as keeping a money journal and enlisting the aid of a mentor—a woman who was a brilliant money manager and who had incredible insight into the stock market. She learned that she was a classic example of a conflicted investor. She constructed a personal money timeline, and it became evident that she was trying too hard to avoid repeating the mistakes her parents had made.

Alice benefited greatly from her counseling. Over the next two years she became more assertive and decided to pursue the economist position if the firm was still willing to support her. She had learned to change the distance between herself and her money. In the beginning, she had to learn to let money flow out of both her mind (concentrate less on money) and pocket (not hang on to it too tightly). Eventually she was able to spend more freely. She started shopping in the better stores and took pleasure buying nice clothes for herself and her daughter.

Alice's professional life improved as well. She found the courage to trade bonds, and was quite good at it. She kept money flowing both long and short. It should come as no surprise that as her success increased, she found that money was on her mind less often.

THE DISTANCE YOU CHOOSE DEPENDS ON THE INVESTOR YOU ARE

Alice was a conflicted investor, and she needed to break out of her old pattern of holding on to the beliefs and fears dictated by her parents. Her breakout resulted in a new relationship between Alice and her money—a new distance between the two. This pattern is typical of a conflicted investor, who often suffers from a lack of balance between the inflow and outflow of money. Conflicted investors are either always saving or always spending. They never use one to offset the other: There is no middle ground. This type of investor needs to turn the "zero-sum" game into a profitable one by having money flow in and out at the same time.

Consumed or revenging investors, who are always in the market, may find that they allow money to flow out too often. They would benefit by holding on to money a little tighter, keeping it closer to home. Perhaps they should decrease their trading activity, which would allow them to maintain more cash assets. Or they could try investing in tangible items such as real estate, art, gold and silver, and rare coins—things rather than more abstract trading vehicles. And, keeping a healthy balance in a savings account will provide them with a feeling of security as well. In other words, revenging investors should attempt to get a bit closer to their money.

Depressed investors need cash flow of any kind. Something has to get them unstuck from the quicksand of their depression. Perhaps a number of small investments in a variety of deals might "spark" them; they, too, need to bridge the distance between themselves and their money.

Obsessed or fussy investors have to let money flow through their hands. Whether it is into their pockets or into their investments, they have to let it go. In many cases, they're too close to their money: They count and must account for every nickel they spend. Backing away from their dollars—perhaps by vowing to invest an affordable amount on a regular basis—will help this investor literally move off the dime.

Paranoid investors may need to take multiple positions with respect to their money because they have trusted no one with anything. They've lost all perspective because they, like fussy investors, are too close to their money. They need to back up, and the way to back up is by taking baby steps in the direction of trust— testing their paranoia by making small trades and investments. When paranoid investors find that no one has betrayed them, their perspective toward money will start to become more realistic.

Case Study
George R., The Paralyzed Money Manager

Achieving a proper distance between yourself and your money is a necessity whether you're a professional or a part-time trader. George learned this lesson the hard way. George was raised in a upper-middle-class family in the suburbs of Cleveland. He attended college at Rochester, a large, private, liberal arts university in upstate New York. He did very well in school, and after earning an MBA, he took his first job at a large Manhattan bank as a loan manager. For several years, George diligently worked his way up the corporate ladder.

In the early 1980s, when corporations began issuing "junk bonds," George moved into the fixed income security division of the bank and quickly learned how to assess corporate assets and liabilities. When his bank established a new mergers and acquisitions division, George was asked to head it because of his expertise in evaluating corporate assets.

George did very well in the various positions he was given, earning high praise and sizable bonuses. In the late 1980s, he was offered a position with a large insurance agency as a top manager of its junk bond portfolio and investments. He worked hard and did well until the junk bond market fell apart and he was left to pick up the pieces with a much reduced staff. The annual bonuses and frequent praise dried up rather quickly.

George had extensive knowledge about and experience in the markets. He had an exquisite feel for the credit markets and interest rate movements. He also had an uncanny knack for analyzing a company's potential for long-term growth. Although most of his own investment consisted of various 401(k) plans and company stock options, he had a working knowledge of the options and futures markets. He decided to try his hand at trading T-bond futures but was unsuccessful. He attributed this failure to "knowing too much," telling his friends that "I feel like I suffer from information overload. Sometimes I know so much that I get paralyzed and can't do anything for myself in the markets."

A closer look at George's general makeup revealed him to be a "revenging" trader. When things didn't go his way in the T-bond market, he didn't know how to let go. Although he had learned that sometimes it was necessary to "cut your losses" in the junk bond market, he had never mastered the task when it came to his own T-bond trading. Inevitably, he would make another trade to "get even." When that didn't work out, he would abandon the market entirely.

George would frequently have dreams that were relevant to his current trading situation, but he never paid attention to them. These dreams usually consisted of "trios" and were generally ridden with sexual innuendos. For example, he would dream of being willingly seduced by a woman, even though he was married. Or, he would dream of driving in his Corvette and chasing a woman in a Porsche. In the dream, he seemed to be constantly shifting gears and so could never catch up with the elusive woman in the Porsche. George would be visited by these dreams when he was in the midst of making trading decisions, but he hadn't learned the important of factoring dreams into such decisions.

Ironically, the tremendous amount of knowledge that George possessed would have been of great help to him if only he had understood the dynamics of his revenging profile. Then he would have been able to interpret the meanings of his dreams and use them to the fullest. He would have been able to institute measures to prevent or counteract his "getting even" tendencies. Even drafting a simple personal money timeline would have been a step in the right direction. With the proper mental distance from his money, George would have been a much more successful investor.

SELF-KNOWLEDGE: THE INSIDE EDGE

If someone as financially sophisticated as George has failed to find the proper distance between his mind and his money, then you can be assured this problem is widespread. No matter how much inside information you possess, without establishing this distance, you lack an inside edge. The key to successful trading and investing resides within your mind. If you're like George, intoxicated by information overload, you'll find yourself making investment decisions under the influence—the influence of how your mind relates to your money.

The most successful investors do have an edge. But it's not the types of edge you typically hear about: classified information, a foolproof system, a genius broker. Their edge is self-knowledge: Whether instinctively or through self-analysis, they recognize their psychological profiles and the advantages and disadvantages those profiles confer. As a result, their investment and trading strategies are based on marketplace realities, not mind-spun illusions.

FINAL MENTAL NOTES

Establishing the optimal investing distance isn't easy. Though everything in this book has been designed to facilitate your efforts in this direction, you're probably going to encounter some obstacles as you adjust to the mind-over-money philosophy. During the adjustment period, the following mental notes should prove helpful:

- *Mental Note 1.* Expect to keep making the same mistakes over and over again. However, as time goes on, they should decrease in frequency, severity, and expense. Furthermore, you should try to correct them while maintaining a high level of self-confidence. Don't be discouraged: A lifelong mind-set cannot be erased in a week or two. You will sometimes slip back into old patterns or habits, but "breaking out" of these habits will become easier with time and effort.

- *Mental Note 2.* As you learn and grow, you will find it increasingly difficult to believe the things that you once did. As your income and success increase, you will look back and be amazed at your naiveté. But remember, you were not naive, but simply operating on an unlevel playing field. Getting in touch with who you are as a person and an investor, acquiring the tools that enable you to identify and monitor the investor inside you—all these things level the playing field.

- *Mental Note 3.* Expect new risks and opportunities. As you achieve the distance you seek, you'll gradually find yourself confronted by fresh investing and trading decisions. When you become aware of your money mind-set, you may have trouble recognizing familiar markets, systems, newsletters, and so on. Things will have changed because your perspective has changed. Don't let yourself become disoriented. Rather, accept the changes you see as natural and ongoing. No matter what psychological type you might be, relax and enjoy your new perspective.

As you break out of the mental constraints that inhibited your relationship with money, remember that the ideas and techniques we've discussed will not instantly become part of your investing/trading persona. It is going to take time and attention. During the course of your investing career, you may have read many books, hundreds of newsletters and newspapers, attended several seminars, listened to cassette tapes, and watched countless television programs on how to invest or trade better. Think of all the time involved. It's a process, and any process takes a while to master and take hold.

But the time invested in these techniques will pay off, sooner as well as later. At first, their only impact might be to alert you that a disastrous trade is about to happen. Over time, they will help you with your investment/trading decisions.

What we advocate is relatively simple. You don't need any special financial skills or experience to make our methods pay off. You just need to follow the steps we've outlined in this book:

- Determine what type of investor you are.
- Keep your journal faithfully.
- Construct a timeline.
- Pay attention to your dreams and fantasies and apply them to your current trading moves.
- Find helpful people.
- Pace yourself to stay alert and refreshed.
- Identify your "next level up."
- Pinpoint your position with respect to the flow of money in and out of your life, keeping a mentally healthy distance.

If you follow these and other recommendations we've made, are you guaranteed fame and fortune? Of course not. You can no more "rig" your mind to make you a lot of money than you can rig the stock market. What you can do, however, is turn a major investing disadvantage into an advantage.

The beauty of this approach is that it's egalitarian: You can use it whether you're a professional or a part-timer, whether you're trading stocks, bonds, or commodities, whether you're risking a lot of money or a little, whether you subscribe to System B or Method R. As long as you have a mind, and as long as it's open, you can train it to make wise and more beneficial decisions about how you invest your money.

APPENDIX A

Small Investors Survey

This survey consists of two parts: (1) Rate your answer on the 0–7 scale at the right of each question; (2) provide short answers. The whole survey shouldn't take more than about 5 minutes. Thank you.

Before you start, please list your age _____ and sex _____.

Part I
In the blank provided, rate each statement from 0 to 7, 0 being not true at all and 7 being very true.

1. Investing/trading is a large part of my life.   _____

2. I have been betrayed by my broker.   _____

3. I have been disappointed by my systems.   _____

4. I have felt relieved after a loss.   _____

5. I enter trades/investments with a lot of energy.   _____

6. I have felt anxious after a successful trade/ investment.   _____

7. Frequently unwanted thoughts about my trades/investments come into my mind. _____

8. I can beat the market. _____

9. I become attached to a trade or investment. _____

10. I am friends with my broker and/or other investors. _____

11. Bad trades/investments enrage me. _____

12. Worries about trades/investments repeat themselves in my mind. _____

13. I take vacations from investing/trading and don't think about it when I'm away. _____

14. I pull out of losing trades. _____

15. I stick with my system/plan, no matter what the loss. _____

16. I am burned out with trading/investing. _____

17. I will become wealthy from trading or investing. _____

18. I recheck many times to see if my trade or investment was bought or sold. _____

19. I am aware of the specific profit I can make from a trade/investment. _____

20. I am a successful investor/trader. _____

21. I am a happy person. _____

22. I am a content person. _____

23. I am a very orderly person. _____

24. I am at odds with myself when I invest/trade. _____

25. I have incurred large debts from investments/trades. _____

26. Investing/trading has interfered with my social life. _____

27. Investing/trading has interfered with my work life. _____

28. Investing/trading has affected my health. _____

29. I am spontaneous in my investing/trading decisions. _____

30. Some might describe me as a depressed type. _____

31. I think drugs or medications have improved my trading/investing. _____

32. My social relationships center around finance/investing. _____

33. I am competitive. _____

34. I calculate out the risk/loss of each potential trade/investment. _____

35. Money is not important to me. _____

Part II

Fill in a short answer in the blank provided after each statement.

1. My three strengths as a person are _____

2. My three weaknesses as a person are _____

3. My father's attitude toward money was _____

4. My mother's attitude toward money was _____

5. Investing in my family was _____

6. My two major memories from childhood are _____

7. The biggest problem I have in life is _____

8. The major problem I keep repeating again and again in my life is _____

   _____

9. I am unhappy with myself investing/trading when _____

   _____

10. My major role model for investing/trading has been _____

   _____

11. I see myself as someone who (please give two- to three-sentence description).

   _____

   _____

Professional Investors Survey

Survey
In the blank provided, please rate the following on a scale of 0 through 10: 0 = N/A, 1–3 = Seldom, 4–6 = Occasional, 7–8 = Often, 9–10 = Frequent.

1. Psychological/personal factors have worked against me in my trading/investing success at some time in my career. _____

2. I consider myself a successful trader/investor. _____

3. The psychological obstacles that have worked against my success in the past or present include:

   a. Being to *obsessive* (*overly* concerned with irrelevant details). _____

   b. Being *overly cautious* or paranoid (worrying too much about getting hurt). _____

   c. Being too *consumed*—needing to get even (always in the market). _____

d. Getting too *depressed* (out of energy, burned out, poor concentration). _____

e. Being *overly competitive* (tie my self-image too much to winning each trade or investment). _____

f. Being *conflicted*—feeling ambivalent, anxious, uncertain about decisions. _____

4. Role models or mentors have been helpful to me in becoming more successful. _____

5. My role model/mentor for trading/investing was/is:

(Fill in the blank) _____

6. The following tools/techniques have helped me cope with the psychological obstacles to my successful trading/investing:

a. Keeping a *journal:* Writing thoughts down along with charts or other kinds of notes. _____

b. *Confiding* in someone. _____

c. Counseling or psychotherapy. _____

d. Paying more attention to my emotions and/or dreams. _____

e. Identifying and keeping track of recurrent patterns of my successful and unsuccessful behaviors. _____

f. Finding different ways to use my talents. _____

g. Seeking out helpful people. _____

h. Taking more vacations/breaks from trading investing. _____

i. Finding a mentor. _____

j. Changing my relationships with family or spouse. _____

k. Forming strategic alliances (investing/trading partners, etc). _____

Comments: (Please comment on your views on how psychological factors influence trading/investing. Have you seen this in your clients? How so?)

_____

_____

_____

_____

Index